CARRIE McDONNALL

with KRISTIN BILLERBECK

FACING TERROR

The *true story* of how
an American couple paid the ultimate
price because of their love of Muslim people.

INTEGRITY®
PUBLISHERS
Nashville

Published by Integrity Publishers, a division of Integrity Media, Inc., 5250 Virginia Way, Suite 110, Brentwood, TN 37027.

HELPING PEOPLE WORLDWIDE EXPERIENCE *the* MANIFEST PRESENCE *of* GOD.

Published in association with Yates & Yates, LLP, Attorneys and Literary Agents, Orange, California.

Some of the names, places, and identifying details mentioned in this book have been changed to protect the individuals involved. These instances will be identified by an asterisk next to the text.

Scripture quotations are taken from the following sources: The Holy Bible, New International Version® (NIV®). Copyright © 1973, 1978, 1984 by International Bible Society. Used by permission of Zondervan. All rights reserved. The Message (MSG) by Eugene H. Peterson. Copyright © 1993, 1994, 1995, 1996, 2000, 2001, 2002. Used by permission of NavPress Publishing Group. All rights reserved.

Cover Design: Benjamin Kinzer, Mark Mickel, Terra Petersen
        Brand Navigation, LLC | www.brandnavigation.com
Author Cover Photograph: King Harrell Photography
Cover Imates: Veer & Corbis
Interior Design: Inside Out Design & Typesetting; Fort Worth, Texas

Library of Congress Cataloging-in-Publication Data

McDonnall, Carrie.
  Facing terror / Carrie McDonnall.
    p. cm.
Summary: "The true story of how an American couple paid the ultimate price because of their love of Muslim people"—Provided by publisher.

ISBN 1-59145-343-7 (hardcover)

1. McDonnall, David, d. 2004. 2. McDonnall, Carrie. 3. Missionaries—Biography.
4. Missions to Muslims. 5. Missions—Iraq. 6. Missions—Middle East. I. Title.

BV2626.M39M33 2005
266'.61'092—dc22   2005014647

Printed in the United States of America
05 06 07 08 BVG 9 8 7 6 5 4 3 2 1

Dedication

This book is dedicated to the life and memory of
my best friend, my husband, and my love . . . David McDonnall.
You lived a joyous life, and I am thankful and honored that I not
only got to experience such joy and love, but that it
spilled into and has overflowed my life.

I love you more . . .
I love you most . . .

To the men and women who unashamedly and obediently run head-
long into the darkness of this world to live out a story that is filled
with love, grace, and forgiveness.
Thank you for your sacrifice.

*I will praise you, O LORD, among the nations;
I will sing of you among the peoples.*

*For great is your love, higher than the heavens;
your faithfulness reaches to the skies.*

*Be exalted, O God, above the heavens,
and let your glory be over all the earth.*

Psalm 108:3–5 (NIV)

Contents

Foreword

Books were piled sky high on my back porch table. I was so engrossed in writing that the phone startled me.

"Mom?" A mother can judge her child's state of mind with one word over a telephone line.

"What is it, darling?" I could tell something was wrong, and I was already up on my feet at full maternal attention. My oldest daughter and her husband were serving in ministry in the United Kingdom, and I rarely talked to her at that time of day. Between sobs, Amanda told me that a missionary couple she and her husband were very close to had been killed. Larry and Jean Elliott had served as missionaries in Honduras for twenty-five years. Curt and Amanda fell head over heels in love with them on a mission trip and had never lost touch. I met the Elliotts a few months earlier when they attended one of our Bible studies in Houston—I could tell immediately why Amanda and Curt loved them so much.

The Elliotts' task in Honduras was complete, and they were awaiting a new assignment. After twenty-five years of faithful service they could have easily retired—but that wasn't their style. Somewhere along the way they probably decided they'd serve on the field right up to the end. And that's exactly what they did—in Iraq.

I could hardly fathom what Amanda described to me. Their car had been sprayed with automatic weapons fire by insurgents in Mosul, Iraq, and they died instantly.

"Amanda, you said there were five people in the car. Do you know the names of the other three?" My heart was pounding. I have been deeply involved with missions and missionaries for years, and I feared hearing the names of other friends like the Elliotts.

"No, ma'am, but I know they were also missionaries."

My stomach grew tight at the thought of whom the others were, but finding out would have to wait. I did everything I could from across a deep ocean to comfort my child. The loss of her friends was bad enough, but the violent way they died was almost more than she could handle. "Sudden glory, Amanda. Sudden glory! One second the Elliotts were toiling and serving, and the next second they saw the face of the One they poured out their lives to share. Imagine it, Amanda. Sudden glory!"

She sobbed and my heart broke. Young adult or not, she was my child, my firstborn, and I hated for her to experience the meanness of this world. I promised to find out everything I could and call her back. Even now, the tears sting in my eyes as I recall hanging up quickly before bursting into my own sobs. I cried what I could not speak: "Precious in the sight of the Lord is the death of his saints" (Psalm 116:15 NIV).

I turned on the television and started flipping through the channels looking for some news of the attack. Within hours the story broke: "Four dead, one survivor." When I heard the names of the other three missionaries, I tried to place them. I've had enough involvement with missionaries through friendships, conferences, and prayer that the names could have had a familiar ring for any number of reasons. I spent a fretful night thinking about the families of the missionaries as well as the staff of the missionary agency. I hardly shut my eyes that night.

The next morning I hurried out the door before dawn to grab the newspaper. The attack was front-page news. I studied the pictures of the five missionaries—the Elliotts, Karen Watson, and David and Carrie McDonnall. I said to my husband, Keith, "I don't know David McDonnall but I am almost certain I know his young wife. For the life of me, though, I don't recognize her name." Later I learned that the press listed her by her given name and I'd known her by a nickname. Staring at her picture and aching with compassion, I had no idea what she would come to mean to me.

Soon my phone was ringing off the wall. The Christian evangelical world is a small world, really. Tragedy comes and we find out just how closely connected we are. If we don't know one another personally, we invariably have mutual friends or associations. First Corinthians 12 describes all Christians as one body—*the body of Christ*: "If one part suffers, every part suffers with it." The news of the attack in Iraq stretched across the globe like ligaments connecting scattered bones. Christians of all kinds grieved as one violently injured body. In only days, Carrie would become a living picture of that body to me.

Lee Sizemore, the producer of our video Bible studies, called me. "Did you recognize the young woman who survived? She was with us in the small group that accompanied you on all the on-location teachings in the Holy Land. They called her by a different name on the news but I know that's her." Several years earlier we'd taken a group of eight hundred people to Israel as the studio audience for the taping of *Jesus the One and Only*. A handful of women had accompanied the camera crew and me for eleven small group teach-ings in various on-site locations. Most of them were young women who were serving in one capacity or another in the Middle East. They were so far from home that we'd wanted to do anything we could to embrace them and invest in them while we were there.

Lee's call supplied the missing piece of the puzzle, and I recalled the connection vividly. Soon after arriving at the ministry office, I put a video of one of the teaching segments into the player and watched Carrie closely. I touched the screen as if to somehow convey comfort to her. The news said she sustained terrible injuries. Fighting back tears, I wondered whether or not the young woman behind that lively expression would have the courage to survive such suffering and loss. I learned of her survival, and her courage, in a way I'll never forget.

Within days, my office received a phone call with this message: "Carrie McDonnall has been transferred privately to a hospital in the Dallas area. She is conscious and communicating. She wonders if she might talk to you."

No words can express the wave of humility and astonishment that overtook me. You don't have to pray about some things. You simply know what God wants you to do. "Yes," I replied, "absolutely. Book a flight." On the morning of Tuesday, April 1, 2004, a friend and I boarded a plane for the short hop to Dallas.

My mind was spinning. I had no idea what to expect or exactly why I'd been summoned, but I was certain to be embarrassingly out of my league. The only time I'd felt less equipped in all my life was on a trip to New York City to minister to grieving people after September 11. In twenty years of ministry, I'd been around plenty of people with deep emotional wounds but never at the bedside of anyone who'd been shot—much less shot multiple times. I'd traveled to third world countries on a number of occasions for ministry but never sustained a scratch for the cause of Christ. What would a lightweight like me have to say to someone who had almost paid the ultimate price for faithfulness to Christ?

I had been instructed to call Carrie's mom, Margaret, as we made our way from the airport to the hospital. I wasn't sure what to say when she answered. Even though I'd been invited to come and see Carrie, I knew the line would be fine between offering support and intruding into a sacred situation. From the time the news broke and the connection was made, I'd wondered repeatedly how Carrie's mom must be handling this. I'm a mother with daughters only a few years younger than Carrie. My children are serving in ministries that could take them anywhere on earth. They have been taught to follow hard after Jesus, and I wondered how I'd feel if they followed Him into gunfire or into widowhood in their mid-twenties.

Margaret answered the phone with a warmth that invited an outsider onto the holy ground of their private lives. That phone call began a sweet friendship between two moms.

I remember exactly where my friend Tammie and I parked at the hospital and every step we took toward the door. The faces of strangers we passed as we crossed the street are still oddly sketched on my mind. Everything seemed to be in slow motion as if my mind took extra time to permanently record the details. We exchanged few words on the elevator ride to Carrie's floor but agreed she'd wait in the waiting room while I went in to meet Carrie. (An hour later, when Carrie and Margaret discovered my friend was in the waiting room, they insisted I go and get her. That's the kind of people they are.)

I tapped on the hospital room door and wondered if they heard it over my pounding heart. I wanted to be a blessing but couldn't imagine how. When Margaret opened the door, we hugged as if we'd known one another forever. I saw Carrie's older sister, Jennifer, sitting pensively in a chair just behind the door. Then my attention was drawn to the hospital bed in the center of the cramped room. I wish I could adequately describe the dichotomy that, at that moment, was Carrie McDonnall.

Carrie's precious body was broken in so many places, but her countenance was welcoming and radiant. *And that hair.* I will smile at the thought of it for the rest of my days. It may have been the most beautiful Texas mane I've ever seen, ironically sitting atop the most broken body I'd ever seen. Had she not been tied down to every conceivable medical contraption, you'd have thought she'd dropped by a salon that morning for a fresh cut and blow dry. Jennifer is a hair stylist and had fixed Carrie's hair just that morning. She looked beautiful.

I am a Southern woman and, to the dismay of many newcomers, we rarely greet a soul we don't hug. But for the life of me, I couldn't find an uninjured place on Carrie to hug. So, I hugged her hair. She'd made a space for me in a chair right beside her bed. I'm at a loss to employ any other word than surreal to describe the next several hours. How in the world anyone could sustain such injuries and live is testimony by itself that God is alive and intentional.

Though Carrie would later remember little of our conversation, she spoke with absolute clarity that day. She described the events that you will read about as she unfolds her story in the pages of this book. Like me, you will probably shake your head and wonder how in the world anyone could live to tell it. This young widow also spoke of her beloved David and her inability to fathom that he was gone. He'd seemed so alive the last time she saw him and so concerned that her life, rather than his, was in jeopardy.

Ultimately, she articulated the reasons why she'd asked me to come. While in the hospital in Dallas, she had experienced consistent visions and heard the sounds of heavenly praises—and wanted to know what they meant. Were they trauma-induced hallucinations or gifts from God?

I believe everything Carrie saw and heard was congruent with Scripture. I never had a moment's doubt that God entrusted those precious sights and sounds to His suffering servant. Strangely, I left the room that day loving Him more than ever. I knew hard days were ahead for Carrie, but I also knew she'd experienced the presence and glory of God in ways few of us will this side of heaven. In the Sermon on the Mount, Jesus declares those who mourn "blessed" and promises them divine comfort. To all who willingly receive, God's comfort is sure—but His ways of extending it may be as unique as the one who is in need.

Carrie's injuries were extensive and the circumstances of her loss unimaginable. Romans 8:18 (NIV) says, "I consider that our present sufferings are not worth comparing with the glory that will be revealed in us." I can only hope I'm standing close by in heaven when God reveals His glory in Carrie McDonnall and others like her. What more could they have offered Him? "They did not love their lives so much as to shrink from death" (Revelation 12:11 NIV). Great is their reward.

—BETH MOORE

PROLOGUE

> "I LOVE telling people about the best thing in my life. I don't have any hesitations in sharing it . . . . Now, I don't understand everything, I *certainly* have plenty of questions, but I am confident that He knows all and He has all the answers. Until we meet and all is revealed, I will keep running the race and keep pressing on toward the goal, relying fully on His strength, which so powerfully works in me, and being confident that He will be faithful to complete the work that He has begun in me."

> *David McDonnall in an e-mail to Carrie, October 1, 2000*

Iraq is a land of modern mystery, a land of ancient history. Amorites, Assyrians, Chaldeans, Babylonians, Jews, Christians, Muslims—all have roots running to this intriguing land. Traditionally, it's said to be the site of the Garden of Eden. Factually, it is the land of Nineveh, of "Jonah and the Whale" fame, of Ur (Abraham's hometown), and Babylon with its hanging gardens, one of the seven wonders of the ancient world. Iraq is an archaeologist's dream, where the soil and sand hide untold secrets yet to be revealed.

My husband, David, and I were certainly attracted to the mysteries of Iraq. We had lived in the Middle East but Iraq was the one country that remained off-limits. Once, on a trip to Amman, Jordan, we went as far east as we could to where Jordan meets Iraq. We stared in awe at the sealed border and wondered, "Will God ever open the door there?"

He did, obviously, with the fall of Baghdad. We made a short-term trip into the country, working on a school for displaced peoples. Not long after, we would call the country our home. We lived in northern Iraq for four months before God called my husband home with fellow missionaries Larry and Jean Elliott and Karen Watson. I returned to America, the sole survivor of a tragic day. At some point, I hope to go back to the Middle East. I need closure. And I need to restore my faith in those Arab friends I grew to love so much. But for now, I deal with the pain I encountered in Iraq and work on moving forward. I will never be the same, but I believe, by the grace of God, that I will be better.

CHAPTER ONE

The Road into Mosul, Iraq

March 15, 2004

Good morning. Credentials." The Kurd soldier's gaze was warm and friendly. The last terrorist checkpoint in the Kurdish land in northern Iraq offered a sense of security before entering the more dangerous open roads of Iraq. We'd been through this checkpoint several times, and the soldiers were getting to know us and had come to recognize our vehicle and our purpose.

The soldiers tried speaking in Kurdish, but when David replied in Arabic, they switched to that more common language. We weren't asked to get out of the car, but they did make the customary checks of the inside of the vehicle. We were Caucasians, and as such, the Kurdish soldiers knew we were prime targets. So they took extra effort to speed us through the checkpoint. I'm certain the always-polite soldiers wondered about the sanity of our group of five Americans leaving the safety of the Kurdish area—but they never voiced their concern. And it wouldn't have stopped us had they done so. We knew perfectly well what we faced each day.

The Iraqi checkpoints were generally commercial in nature, crowded with young boys selling candy bars, bananas, cigarettes, and sometimes, foreign money. With cars stopped, these boys had a lucrative business, feeding hungry passengers as they waited for the bureaucratic wheels to turn at the checkpoint. David and I had become familiar targets to the youthful merchants. They knew to hit us up on the way back, when we were usually famished from the day's work. We kept small change to buy candy bars and bananas from them. This often would serve as a missed meal, since we'd get involved in our work and forget to eat. Other times, we did it simply to help out these young entrepreneurs as they tested the waters of the free market.

We had a particular child we tried to purchase from, since he was younger and the older boys would often push him around. My heart just leapt at the sight of this little boy. He always wore the same sweater and pants, and though we'd traveled the road several different times during the months, there he would be, every time, in his same, familiar outfit. He knew we would wait for him, and he'd run up to our car, pushing past his older competitors. After the sale, he would wave his money in victory. The older boys would laugh at his delight and then push past him to try and offer us more of the same fare.

It was quite a game, and it brought us joy to see his small triumph. Naturally, we would try to buy something different from the other kids, too—all this commerce taking place through the truck windows while we inched slowly forward toward the guards. We looked forward to our contacts at the checkpoint, but on this day we were anxious to get through.

This was the last day that Larry and Jean Elliott and Karen Watson would be with David and me. Before they returned to Baghdad the following day, we wanted them to help us with an assessment at an IDP (Internally Displaced Peoples) camp we'd had a hard time locating. We valued their expertise and wanted the benefit of their experience as we visited the IDP camp.

We'd been in contact with the U.S. Army several times trying to learn the exact location of the camp but without success. It was the kind of frustration you learn to live with in a war-torn country— sometimes the right and left hands don't communicate well. On this particular day we were going to visit the army base in person to try to obtain directions to the camp.

The checkpoint seemed unusually long that day. We were anxious to get this project behind us and move on to a new one waiting on the horizon. And all five of us were ready for a break mentally. The discovery and assessment trips we'd taken into Mosul and the surrounding areas in the last weeks had been exhausting, and we were ready to regroup.

As we were released from the checkpoint, the desert sun blazed down upon us. It was an early spring day, and it never took long for the morning chill to burn off. We were in the high desert of northern Iraq, where rolling hills turn into small mountains that grow ever larger in the neighboring countries of Turkey, Syria, and Iran.

My own gaze focused on the jutting mountains in the distance, and I shivered. Later I wondered if it was a premonition, but at the time I assumed it was only the thought of the snow in winter and how it made the landscape so beautiful in the spring. Lush waterfalls and lovely wildflowers created a canvas of color, dotted by the young goats and lambs of the season. It should have seemed idyllic, but the ominous sense of danger was never more than a thought away.

We'd made this trip many times in the recent past. In the two weeks Karen Watson had stayed with us we had traveled all over, even into Mosul a few times with her and the Elliotts. Because Mosul is beyond the last Kurdish checkpoint, there is more danger associated with the area. Active terrorist groups like *Hamas* and the *Wahhabis*, a violent, radical Muslim group, keep Mosul from flourishing or setting up a permanent infrastructure. David's and my overall goal in being in Iraq, as well as the Elliotts' and Karen's, was to work with those Iraqis who craved a sense of normalcy and wanted their country to move forward.

Radical Islam does not represent the majority of Muslims, not even in Iraq. Therefore, we didn't have the same level of fear that many who aren't familiar with the region would. This was before the vicious beheadings, kidnappings, and random killings began. Most Iraqis were thankful for our services and did what they could to help us in return. The Kurds had a long history of working with NGOs (Non-Governmental Organizations). However, the radicals do not want any outside groups to succeed, regardless of which people group they're working to help. The radicals want *jihad*, and therefore are against any group that moves Iraq and the Muslims toward being part of the world community of nations. So, as we headed to the army base, we were on guard but determined not to allow fear to paralyze us.

As dangerous as traveling *near* Mosul was, David and I had actually been trying to move *into* Mosul to work with Arab Sunni Muslims in that area. Contrary to what you see in the media, the Sunnis aren't all monsters in *khafias* (the traditional Arab head-wrapping). Most of them are generous, hospitable spirits in need of the Lord, and David's love for them was unparalleled in this world. David felt as at-home among the Sunnis as he would in his beloved Colorado.

In northern Iraq, where Mosul is located, clean water is always an issue because the government never managed to set up a solid utility infrastructure: electricity and pure water. As the hot, dry summer approached, water would be a top priority for those in transient homes, like the IDP camp to which we were headed. Our mission team was based in the north for exactly this purpose: to help provide clean water and other necessities to displaced peoples.

Our combined humanitarian experience prepared us for the work. David had traveled in northern and eastern Sudan to assess water in the villages, and I had worked for two years in a foster home in Israel. Larry and Jean Elliott had been stationed in Honduras for twenty-five years, and specialized in water systems to bring the precious liquid to outlying areas. Karen Watson had been one of the first missionaries into Iraq, though she had recently been studying Arabic in another country. She had left Iraq after a close call with a bomb a few months prior but now was making arrangements to move back permanently and actually had all her belongings waiting for her in Baghdad.

So the mission field was not foreign to any of us. We knew the danger we faced every day, especially in post-Saddam Iraq, but we still heeded God's call. Any of us could be hit by a bus back home in America. But on this day God had called us to northern Iraq, and that is where we were determined to serve. Although David and I had only recently met the Elliotts and Karen, we quickly gelled into a team.

Beyond the Kurdish checkpoint the ride was relatively silent. We knew the roads were increasingly unsafe the further we were from the Kurdish territory. Drive-by ambushes, roadside bombs (the infamous IEDs—Improvised Explosive Devices), or other terrorist scenarios were always a possibility. Iraq is a theater of war without front lines. There is no place where one ever feels completely safe. We honored that reality as we drove in silence toward the army base.

The Kurdish people are the world's largest ethnic group without a country to call their own. They have their own territory in what is referred to as Kurdistan in northern Iraq. Although they have yet to be legally recognized by other countries, they have remained on good terms with American forces and they are well-governed by their own opposing political parties (think Democrat and Republican). Their portion of Iraq is currently light-years ahead of neighboring areas in terms of a functioning society. Our plan that day was to be back in the relative safety of the Kurdish territory well before nightfall.

We felt relief as we approached the U.S. Army base, as it meant a chance to get off the roads. Coalition forces may have secured many cities and areas, but the roads between them remain a huge concern for Iraq's future.

Our goal at the army base was to get the exact GPS (Global Positioning Satellite) coordinates for the IDP camp we were assessing that day. We would then use our own hand-held GPS unit to find the displaced peoples we were searching for. CMOC, the Civil Military Operations Center, is the branch of the army that works with charities and other non-governmental organizations. With the U.N. having fled Iraq, the work of NGOs became more important in providing relief for those people affected by the ravages of Iraq's internal strife and the war. Coordination for NGO relief efforts used to be handled independently by individual civilian groups, but as northern Iraq became increasingly more violent it was clear that the military would have to intervene. The CMOC kept a list of all NGO activities and tried to coordinate their efforts.

Being a small team, David and I generally worked with short-term visiting teams and took the small jobs, those too small for the army or other NGOs to handle. Our military contacts on the base seemed genuinely excited about our taking on the requirements in the area. They knew these displaced peoples had not had their needs assessed properly, and they looked forward to receiving the information our survey would provide.

Once at the military base, we confirmed our goals for the day, and David and I made plans to return at a future time for security tips. We still planned to make our permanent home in Mosul, and needed the safety and security information the military could give us before we made the leap. Obviously, it was still a very unstable city, but David and I hoped eventually to see a sports facility built there, a gathering place for children.

After getting the GPS coordinates, the five of us went on our way and saw no difficulty in making it back to the Kurdish territory before dark. We were upbeat about the prospects of finally reaching our destination given the prior difficulty we'd had in locating the camp.

We were looking for an old, run-down factory. Saddam Hussein had paid many Arabs to move up north and populate the area to provide a protective buffer between Baghdad and his enemies to the north. The Kurdish peoples that populated the area were displaced by Saddam's directives and ended up taking refuge wherever they could. It was like a game of ethnic musical chairs, only on a violent, national scale.

The factory came into sight, and a paved road—a distinct sign of civilization in Iraq—led to two boxy, concrete buildings: one was single-story and the other two-story, both characteristically plain and drab. We spied chickens and sheep, and as experienced relief and development workers, this told us food was not an issue. Clothes hung on a line outside the buildings, which indicated good hygiene. First impression: the buildings and people were clean, and they had food to eat. For humanitarian relief workers, these were very positive and encouraging signs.

We could see women peering out of the windows from behind curtains, so, knowing the customs, Mrs. Elliott, Karen, and I got out of the truck, leaving the men behind. It would have been inappropriate for the men to exit the truck without a man from the community present. An elder woman, probably the sheik's wife, came out to speak to us in Arabic. I spoke just enough Arabic to get by. (David called Arabic the language of heaven because it would take you until eternity to learn it completely.) Karen also spoke enough to understand what was going on, but Mrs. Elliott was at our mercy.

Arab women are beautiful—but very straightforward. They think nothing of telling you to your face you're fat, not as a slight, but just as a matter of fact. They're very affectionate towards one another and will invade your personal space without hesitation. But it is their hospitality I love—it's like nothing you've ever experienced. If you talk for five minutes on the street, they invite you in for tea, and you are their friend for life. Everyone has time for a visit in the Arab world; not to take time is considered an insult and extremely rude. We'd become accustomed to incorporating visits into every aspect of our ministry in the Arab cultures. It was the most enjoyable part of our jobs.

While we talked with the Arab women outside the factory, one of them focused on Mrs. Elliott. The woman just seemed to recognize that Jean Elliott was a kind spirit. She exuded peace and warmth when you were around her, and this Arab woman sidled right up next to her while we spoke. Jean was one of those amazing Christians who spoke a non-verbal language of love regardless of the culture. While we socialized, David and Larry Elliott remained in the truck discussing the state of the camp.

While we spoke, some of the Arab men appeared. David and Mr. Elliott jumped from the truck to greet them, asking if it would be all right for us to join the women. Arab hospitality is such an art form, and this was the proper way to go about it. The Iraqi people are extremely clean, and a house must be prepared for guests at all times since a dirty house reflects poorly upon the husband. (It reminds me of the verse in Proverbs 31 where the husband is respected as an elder at the city gate due, in part, to his wife of noble virtue.) The "house" was wonderfully kept, and the ladies went to work on providing us with something to eat and drink. It always amazed me how Arab women, living in very trying circumstances with relatively scarce resources, could produce tea, bread, fruit, and other refreshments at a moment's notice for the benefit of complete strangers.

The two-story factory had an extravagant lobby with two circular staircases winding up to the second floor living area. Though half the stairs were crumbling, overall the structure was sound and made a good home. Again, our humanitarian mental checklists were being tallied.

We (the three women) were led to the largest of the rooms, which is customary. Most Iraqis sleep on the floor on thick mattress-like pads laid atop traditional Persian-style rugs. During the day, the pads are rolled up and stored against the wall, where they become backrests for those sitting around the periphery of the room, leaning against the wall. We removed our shoes before stepping onto the rug, and we all sat around a kerosene heater, the smell of which one gets used to in the Middle East. The ladies served us hot tea and oven-fresh flat bread.

We realized this must be all they had since guests are usually offered fruit as well. The absence of fruit was the first evidence of what they lacked. It must not have been due to a lack of funds as much as unavailability, since they had money to buy cigarettes, which we were offered. We declined politely, not just because none of us smoke but because we knew that the offer of cigarettes is often a test of morality. Though most Arab women don't smoke, I laughed inside as the older woman bent down and lit her cigarette on the hot flames of the kerosene heater.

All of these women in the home were related in some way, and our ladies' conversation revolved around how they were all related—who was whose wife, cousin, sister, and so on. The connections were dizzying to say the least.

"Where are you from?" they asked in Arabic.

"America. We are here to help with food and water," I answered.

"We need water," the woman answered plainly.

I nodded, saying I'd tell my husband. I didn't know what David was telling the men outside, and I didn't want to make any promises we couldn't keep. We were probably there for another forty-five minutes visiting about our lives and families before we decided we'd better go out and check on the men. Our visit went on longer than we'd expected, and the hour was getting late. It was time to wrap it up if we were going to make the Kurdish checkpoint before dark.

Once outside we saw that the men weren't finished talking, so we took our places in a circle on the opposite side of the yard. We took several pictures with the women and of their home. Just as we were heading to the truck I was surprised by an Iraqi man who was getting into our already full truck with us.

I tried to play the submissive wife, but when I saw him climb into the vehicle, I took David aside: "Honey, why is this man coming with us?" I whispered in English.

"He has more family up the road in need of help. He's just going to show us where they live, and we'll get coordinates," David answered.

I trusted David completely, and if he said the man had good intentions, I believed it wholeheartedly. We drove up the rural road to another complex on our way to Mosul, about five minutes away from the first housing project. Our guest was very excited about the possibility of us helping the rest of his extended family. Since it was getting late, we decided not to make an official assessment—only David and Larry would get out of the truck and make contact with the family.

When we arrived at the settlement, David quickly jumped out, marked the spot on his GPS, and said we'd return later to do a formal assessment. The man who'd come with us left us there, catching another ride back to the original settlement. We were finally on our way back to the protected Kurdish zone, much to my relief. It wasn't the area that frightened me nearly as much as the cover of darkness. Traveling in Iraq as the sun goes down is not recommended. In fact, it's really not done.

At this point on the return to Mosul, we could have turned off and taken one of the many back roads rather than go through town—but we didn't. This is where I have to rely on God's sovereignty or go crazy with "What if?" speculations. What if we hadn't made the additional stop . . . if we had turned onto a back road? What if? What if?

Going straight through Mosul was the most direct route, and the road led us into town near the university, a known hotbed of insurgent activity and angry extremists. Although we hadn't been warned that particular day about the area, we knew the hour was getting late, and the university tended to attract youth committed to *jihad*. It was still light outside, and there was little to worry about with the afternoon bustle and crowds milling about in the street. But as we approached town, my heart raced at the sight of our worst nightmare: *traffic.*

CHAPTER TWO

Downtown Mosul

March 15, 2004—Late Afternoon

As we turned the corner into town, traffic halted, all three haphazard "lanes" of it, and we were locked in between cars. The street was gray with haze from bad air. The stench of sewage filled our truck, even with the windows closed, and I grew antsy, praying for traffic to clear and free us from the virtual cage.

The boxy buildings on either side of the street were covered in a layer of brown dust from the unpaved roads, and everything seemed normal. Businesses were open; people walked along the sidewalks and entered the shops. Curtains blew out of second-story windows over the storefronts. There was movement everywhere, but we were deadlocked in traffic. (One never wants to be boxed into traffic in Iraq for obvious reasons. Even the checkpoints are frightening that way, as most of them are walled, and there's no place to go if someone decides to start shooting.)

As I took in my surroundings, I knew this situation wasn't good, but I tried not to let my nerves show. Before I fully assessed my fear, I felt something sting me. "Ow!" I cried out. Whatever it was stung the top of my ear, and I instinctively reached for it. Clutching my ear, my world suddenly went dark.

I revived fairly quickly, still dizzy, but aware enough to hear David shout, "Get down! Everybody get down!"

My heart raced, but there was nowhere to go and I couldn't heed the warning. I was lost in my confusion and befuddled, not truly feeling everything, not understanding what was happening, only sensing danger. The sting of my ear became a moot point.

Our pickup truck had an extended cab and I was in the back seat with Karen to my left and Mrs. Elliott to my right. David sat in the driver's seat and Mr. Elliott was in the passenger seat. None of us spoke after David's warning. The deafening roar of automatic rifles surrounded us.

It was like living in a nightmare, everything in slow motion. Only the throbbing, pounding explosive noises persisted, and the metallic scent of gunpowder and blood filled my senses. Six men with AK-47s and at least one Uzi submachine gun surrounded our vehicle, their guns raised, firing at will into the vehicle. I felt the constant bite of pain everywhere, as bullets and shrapnel ricocheted off the walls and floor of the truck. There was no escape—the hail of bullets came at us from every direction.

I clasped my eyes shut at the sight of the men. I didn't want to remember their eyes. I didn't want to know who would do this or see the hatred in their expressions. I can't say I was even thinking coherently enough to pray at the time. I was merely watching a movie unfold, unable to grasp what, if anything, I could do. Bullets were raining like white-hot volcanic ash, coming from every crevice. There was nowhere to hide. I couldn't move. I was at the mercy of the terror surrounding our vehicle.

There wasn't even room for me to slink down, and even if there had been, it wouldn't have done any good. The bullets bounced off the floorboards, and my lower legs felt the constant and persistent stinging. I opened my eyes slightly to see David bent down in the driver's seat, he, too, with nowhere to go. By now, recognition had surfaced. I understood what was happening. There was an unreal feeling that our worst fears were coming to pass.

"Jesus, make the bullets stop!" I finally prayed. Then, I blanked out again, enveloped in the safety of the blackness. When I came to, I was the only one awake and the reign of terror had ended. The piercing throbs had stopped, and only silence remained—an eerie, hollow silence. Where there was once a bustling city street, now there was absolutely no sign of life.

People had scattered like cockroaches in the light. Traffic had dissipated, and the shops appeared closed. It was as though a great wind had cleared the street of any humanity, including the traffic jam we were in, and only we remained. Our truck was slowly moving, headed straight for the two-foot high curb, and with David bent unconscious over the steering wheel, I braced for impact as we inched forward.

After we hit the curb with a hard thud, I looked around and took in my environment. Utter devastation lay around me. Mrs. Elliott, my precious friend whose spirit was so universally revered, was gone. I could feel her body slumped against mine, and her breathing had stopped. On my left, Karen was bent over as well, but I could still hear her breathing, ever so faintly. I wanted to check her pulse, but my arms wouldn't budge. I felt like I was encased in mud, powerless to proceed, and not comprehending why. I reasoned that it was better not to wake her anyway, in case she was in pain. I took in the scene as if I was outside looking in. I don't know that I could have handled it otherwise. No one moved, and I didn't know what to think. Was David pretending to be asleep? Had he felt the metal rain like I had?

Then, I caught sight of my hand. It was horrific, drenched in blood, missing fingers, bones visible, so I tried to prop it up over my heart. At that very moment, when my basic first-aid training started to kick in, I heard God whisper to me, "You're going to be fine."

I asked God, "Is my husband alive?"

I remembered how Jesus' disciples would often ask Him questions, the answers to which they really weren't prepared to receive—so I stopped asking, not knowing what the answer might be. We were newlyweds. We had our entire lives in front of us. This is what I focused on rather than face the reality of the devastation surrounding me.

Bullets and metal shrapnel were everywhere—on the floor, lodged in the truck's walls, all over us. Shards of glass covered everything like a crystal snowfall. There was something in my mouth, and I remember hearing it "clink" on the truck floor when I spit it out. Internally I felt something wasn't right, and I couldn't breathe through my nose, though I didn't know why. Mentally, I tried to process what to do, how to proceed—but everything was so blurred.

The street was deathly still. But we were in a neighborhood—there had to be people somewhere. Not that I blamed them for scattering—I would have done the same thing. But it was eerie to feel so utterly alone when I knew there were hundreds of people peering out at us, people who could help if only they would.

"Help me," I tried to say in Arabic. But it was barely a whisper. "Help me!" I said again, trying to yell. I began to see men milling about in the street, but they stayed away. They looked at the scene, but they didn't look at me directly. It was obvious they couldn't hear me. I tried to speak louder, but I couldn't. "Help me," I said again quietly, to no avail. I thought I would bleed to death because I couldn't be heard. They were too far away from the truck.

"Help me," I said again.

At that very moment, David sat straight up in the driver's seat. "Are you hit?" David asked, fully cognizant of our situation.

"Yes," I said. "I'm hit bad, David. I have to get to the hospital." I cried out through jagged breaths. "Are you hit?"

"No," David answered.

I thought, *How could he not be hit?* I saw how bad *I* was, and I was surrounded by Mrs. Elliott and Karen, shattered glass, shrapnel, bullets . . . . Up front, Mr. Elliott looked as though he had died as well. *How could David not be hit?*

He certainly didn't act as if he were wounded. He got out of the truck with determination in his step and began taking charge of the situation. David had a strong and powerful voice. We actually had a signal between us when he would get too loud or animated in conversation. He loved to tell stories and often became so animated people would stare. I would flash our signal and he would immediately tone it down. That loud voice, the one I'd tried many times to lower, would now save my life.

Outside, David looked back towards the truck. I saw the horror in his eyes as he looked at the bullet-riddled truck full of bodies, blood, and shattered glass. But he stopped and looked me straight in the eye with such compassion—I'll never forget it. It was as though he never saw my hand or my bloodied face. David couldn't stand the sight of human blood, but his eyes met mine, saying without speaking, "I'm going to take care of you. Just like I swore I would on our wedding day." With my whole heart I believed that he would. The love and compassion I saw in his eyes said so much about who he was. This man *knew* how to love.

After gazing at me intently, he turned back to the street. "Help us!" David bellowed in Arabic. Immediately, the men milling about came forward. I could hear David rambling in Arabic. He was finding people to help him, rounding people up on the street, and explaining his wife needed to get to the hospital. I closed my eyes in relief. David would handle the situation, and I allowed myself to relax a bit.

I could see that David was losing the color in his face. I thought perhaps it was the sight of me or the signs of shock. Still, I didn't see any blood on him, and I chose to believe what he had said, that he hadn't been hit. I noticed that Karen's breathing beside me became slower and more labored, until it stopped altogether, and I actually *felt* her die. Knowing that Mrs. Elliott was gone, too, I remember thinking, *If I live through this, how will I ever get over being so near to death?* I was literally surrounded by it, drowning in it, and my heart just ached at the thought of such good people coming to this end. One can never imagine experiencing death as close as this, and my heart grieved as much as I could allow while maintaining the determination to survive.

Mrs. Elliott had a spirit that spoke to others through a common, non-verbal language. Mr. Elliott had a hearty laugh that would forever ring in my ears. And Karen was the most charitable soul. I was even wearing a long-sleeved shirt she'd bought on our shopping trip a week ago, which now seemed like an eternity ago. I felt so helpless watching my friends fall away, knowing I couldn't do anything to catch them.

In America, when a fatal event occurs, there are sirens; there's help on the way. But here I knew that help would only come if we searched for it, and I looked at David out on the street trying to find it. I tried to pray but didn't know what to pray. I looked at the remains of my left hand and thought, *This should hurt!* But it didn't. I just felt numb. Seeing my colleagues around me, the victims of such a heartless attack, I couldn't bear to feel anything because emotionally and physically, it was too much to take.

David got back in the truck—I don't know why he did this, perhaps it was the shock—and backed it up and parked it alongside the road. So it looked as though it was parked for a normal trip to the city center, even though it was riddled with bullet holes, and filled with our beloved team now gone on to another place.

"Are we going to the hospital?" I asked.

"We have to get another car," David said calmly. He hopped out of the truck and began talking to the men again. David turned towards me and spoke through the glassless window, "This man is going to take us to the hospital. I have to get *you* to the hospital."

The man David found turned out to be an off-duty Iraqi police officer, and his presence at the scene was truly miraculous. To help in the middle of Mosul was to risk one's own life and limb at the hands of insurgents and bystanders. I'd seen how easy it was to inflame an angry crowd during my time in Israel, and tensions were already high. Finding anyone to help was indeed a miracle; finding an off-duty policeman was simply a divine appointment. But of course, I didn't truly appreciate it at that moment. I needed to get to the hospital but did not want to leave my friends behind. I never had time to feel fear or think of the possibility of the masked gunmen coming back. For that, I'm grateful.

As David got us ready to leave, I looked at him. "We need my purse," I said, thinking of my passport. "We need my purse and the sat [satellite] phone." It's amazing how logic kicks in when you can't stand to feel the emotions. There was so much I knew instinctively: keep my hand elevated, stay awake, keep my passport and a phone with me at all times. Those instincts took over as I got ready to move to the other car.

The Iraqi men who'd agreed to help came around to the door of the truck and looked at me as if to say, *Come on out.* Touching another man's wife was not on their list of things to do that day, especially not a Caucasian woman who clearly was out of her element, amidst a town embroiled with insurgency. And I'm sure the mere sight of me didn't appear inviting. I could still see my bones, see the blood and feel its sticky sensation around me.

"I can't move, David," I said to my husband, rather than addressing the men. I couldn't move any of my limbs, though I still had no idea why. My entire body felt like cement, mired in the truck. "You're going to have to help me out."

Mrs. Elliott was moved out of the way. I remember looking at this precious woman knowing I would never forget the image of her life-less body. I knew her spirit was gone and happy, but to see her here without life, a physical reminder of all that had just happened, was crushing. This worthy woman of God deserved so much better and it devastated me to see her gone, knowing the others were gone too. We knew, coming to Iraq, what we'd signed up for, but obviously we never expected this. We never expected gunmen or to be the subjects of a "soft target" news article. *This felt wrong.*

The men who had come to help were still standing and staring at me, waiting for me to hop out of the truck. In America, we are trained in basic first aid. We know the fundamentals of applying pressure to a wound or not moving someone with a neck injury. Common sense would dictate that I wasn't going anywhere, but the men had no idea what to do. It is not because they are without feeling but because their mores said not to touch another man's wife, espe-cially when the man was standing right beside them. Even in a life-

or-death situation, the culture is innate in the people. Veering from that path is not appropriate, or done, without extreme prodding.

David looked woozy at this point and wavered in his stance. I noticed he was about to fall, and I screamed out, "Catch my husband! Catch my husband!"

The men were able to catch him, but it was clear I needed help from the Iraqi men to move me. I can't remember the last time I used the word "arm" or "leg" in Arabic, but my language skills suddenly sharpened. "My arms and legs don't work," I said in Arabic to the men. "You have to get me out."

One man put his hands under me, and when he grabbed me, I felt every broken bone in my body explode in pain. Every part of me froze—except my vocal chords. My nerves came alive in anguish and I screamed out in agony. The pain engulfed every last square inch of me. My bones felt crushed and in places they had no business being. I felt as though I were in pieces, hanging together by a mere thread. My scream seemed to go on forever, echoing in the silent street. I still had no idea what was wrong with me, but I knew it was serious. Someone held me underneath my leg, and they set me down on the concrete while I tried to recover from the movement.

I was wearing a plain, long, loose skirt, as is Iraqi custom. Even though my skirt was only up to my calf when the men set me down, one of them bent down and pulled my skirt hem down to cover my ankles. I remember crying at this gesture. To think that this man would care about my dignity in such a situation made my heart soar. It was such an act of love, to preserve my modesty—an act reserved for wives or sisters or mothers. That man showed love in the midst of horror, and I'll never forget it because I needed that token to keep me going. I needed to see the good in people at that moment, and it was a direct gift from above.

Arab men are generally not big in stature, and I am not a petite woman. Two men approached to lift me from the sidewalk and I quickly called out in Arabic, "There needs to be three! There needs to be three!" My voice seemed to work fine when pain was involved.

Another man got up the courage to help and lifted me from underneath, holding his arms out straight so no one would think he was touching me in an indecent manner. They put me into a beat-up taxi with four bald tires. The middle guy dropped out at this point, disappearing into the crowd that gathered as though he'd never bothered with me.

I sat in the back seat between the two Arab men who had helped, and as David approached the car with the sat phone, trying to call our boss in Jordan, I saw his coloring was worse. He trembled as he reached for the door and dropped the phone, losing the satellite connection. When David got into the cab, all appeared right again, but I knew he had indeed been hit somewhere. He again called our boss from the sat phone. "Carrie and I have been hit," I heard him say, before he passed out and dropped the phone, losing the connection again.

Now I knew he had been wounded, but I had no idea where or how seriously. But as I saw him lose consciousness, my fear for his life began to mount. David recovered and dialed our boss again. The fact that he got a connection at all while moving was extraordinary, as sat phones in Iraq are about as reliable as a cellular phone in a tunnel. These phones are not the best in reception. We often went to our roof and stood completely still to make our phone calls. The fact that it worked while we were moving, in the middle of town, was miraculous.

My pain was overwhelming at this point, and I don't have a strong recollection of David's next phone call. I was aware his pain was worse than he'd let on, and his symptoms appeared to be having more of an effect. He was increasingly dazed and definitely absent healthy color. My own pain diminished as I thought of David's being hit and worried about his getting to the hospital as well.

"Did you get my purse?" I asked when he got off the phone.

"Someone got it," he said. (I did eventually get it back. Someone must have taken it to the Iraqi police station.)

"Hospital. Get us to the hospital." I croaked out to the taxi driver.

"Police station," he countered.

Then David started to argue for the hospital as well.

The taxi driver was adamant. He knew we were still in danger. "Police station!" he argued, not wanting to be responsible if the gunmen came back. It took convincing, but David finally won the argument—right before I felt the car roll to a slow stop.

"What are we doing? Why are we stopping?" I remember shouting. I heard something about gas, and by now my patience was running thin, and pain was having its affect on my personality. "We're stopping for gas?" I exclaimed, incredulous.

"Yes. Yes," the Iraqi taxi driver nodded. "Gas," he repeated in Arabic. I was very weak from loss of blood at this point, but I was certain that if there was *any* gas left in this vehicle, it was enough to get us to the hospital. *It wasn't that far! We'd passed it on our way into town.* Time stood still as I tried to wrap my brain around one more barrier to pain relief. *Let's go, let's go, let's go!*

I hurt everywhere. My legs throbbed and my arms were bloodied with gaping wounds. My face felt different, and I still couldn't breathe well through my nose. I smelled blood, I saw blood, and I was covered in it. I was filthy from the attack, with a layer of the brown dust from the street and small bits of glass still blanketing me. I just wanted relief. I was immune to what was happening around me—cars driving around us, people milling about. I just felt pain, and knew only that the car wasn't moving. And I desperately wanted it to be.

David and the taxi driver got out of the car. David, still pale, though I couldn't see any blood, seemed to be moving okay, but slower than before. David and the taxi driver opened the hood. (Taxis in Iraq are not the Mercedes-Benzes seen in Jordan. They resemble cars only in the fact that they have four wheels, the tires on which are usually lacking any treads.) Apparently, there was a clog in the gas line, and I watched as David and the driver jimmied it with a coat hanger to get gas to the engine.

"*Come on, come on, come on,*" I mumbled. I wished more than ever that I was in America where I could dial 911 and know that policemen, firemen, and EMTs would be there within minutes. Such an infrastructure is not in place in Iraq.

With the men out of the car, I watched as another car came around and slowed near us. I saw recognition flash in the taxi driver's eyes. My heart pounded at the sight of yet another vehicle slowing next to our own. *Had the gunmen come back to finish the job? Or was this more insurgents looking for trouble?* Everyone froze, eyes fixed on the car. At that very second, a large truck full of Iraqi policemen pulled behind them and they sped off. We hadn't called the police, but they were definitely the cavalry that day. I like to think Someone else called them. Now we had security but lacked a working vehicle.

I still couldn't form a prayer. I kept thinking of the Rich Mullins song, "Hold Me, Jesus." And I felt a calming sense that there is power in His Name, so I just kept repeating, "Jesus. Jesus. Jesus."

David heard me, and he started to pray for us. His voice, as it always did, calmed and soothed me. For me, when David was speaking, everything was under control. I relaxed in his leadership and listened to him pray, just like at night before we'd go to sleep.

The police pulled in front of us to provide an escort to the hospital. After a bit more playing with the coat hanger, the cab finally started again and we were on our way.

Just when we thought our path to the hospital was clear—with a working vehicle and a police escort—we still only crawled forward, as if held back by some unseen force. Where once I'd seen a clear road, now I saw only obstacles in our way: people milling about and our view blocked by the large police truck. We moved forward gingerly, waiting as the police escort cleared the road of people. A mob had formed and blocked the police escort's path. I didn't know what the crowd wanted, and I didn't care. I just wanted the road clear, my pain to stop, and help for David. Finally, the police handled the situation, and we crawled towards the hospital. I knew we were close now. We were going to make it!

The cab rolled to a stop in front of the hospital, and David got out, met by two men from the hospital. They propped him up on a makeshift gurney that looked like something left over from World War II, and he disappeared from my view. My Iraqi escorts pulled me out of the car. My body screamed in protest as they flopped me over a sorrier version of David's stretcher. I only had one somewhat working limb, my right leg, and I put as much pressure on it as it would hold.

My left leg was in pieces so I stood on the one "good" leg, unable to use my listless arms, struggling to breathe through my nose. My manners had long since gone. "A little help here!" I screamed in English, thinking to myself, *Can you not see me shot up here?* (I discovered that, when in pain, my thoughts and words became less edifying than they normally were!) I wanted help. I wanted the pain to stop, and I wanted just one person from the mob forming outside the hospital to offer his help.

By now, the men assisting me noticed the mob crowding around, and they were starting to worry about their own safety. That makes complete sense, and I didn't blame them, but I still wondered if the hospital even knew I was out there at the ambulance entrance. Did they think only David was in the car—that only he needed help? I felt exposed and helpless, and while I was angry, the emotions did me little good. I waited, slung over the gurney, hoping and praying someone would come out of the hospital. I prayed that I hadn't gotten this far to be mauled by an angry mob outside the emergency room.

I thought perhaps they'd taken David in because he was the man—of far more importance in the Arab culture. I held out hope that they had indeed seen me in the taxi and were coming back to get me. Looking back, I wonder if the hospital personnel didn't see David's injuries were more serious than any of us noticed.

I knew enough about the current state of Iraq to know I didn't want Iraqi doctors working on us. Unless we were at risk with fatal injuries, surgery or serious medical help was not an option in the hospital. Obviously, Iraq's facilities would not be that of the American military's field hospital. We saw the Iraqi hospital as a stopping-off point—a place to get stabilized before being picked up by the American army and moved to a field hospital.

The sad truth is you don't know if the Iraqi doctors, at least in Mosul, are willing to fight for your survival or help speed your demise. This was known insurgent territory, and one was never completely sure of loyalties. It was more important than ever to stay alert now, though I was so very weary and weak.

We *had* to get to the CSH (Combat Support Hospital) unit. Finally, after waiting in fear, two hospital employees came out where I was waiting on the gurney and brought me into the main emergency room with David. The Iraqi police came in with me, automatic weapons in hand. There was a child in the emergency room, screaming at the top of his lungs. The sight of a battered and bleeding woman, surrounded by policemen with AK-47s at the ready, was more than he could handle. I doubt he'll ever be free of the memory. *Get this kid out of here,* I thought to myself. *Where is the mother?*

An Iraqi hospital has the standard hospital-green walls, and doctors in white coats, but there are obvious signs you're not in an American or other high-tech facility: old wooden cupboards . . . metal cabinets . . . tired twin beds with striped sheets . . . IVs hooked on old metal stands. Everything metal was flaked with rust. The appearance of the facility was not a confidence-booster in terms of the quality of care we might receive.

A female doctor came in and started to look me over and assess the damage. My hands were the most obvious to me, and the doctor soon bound them in wraps without cleaning them. I was covered in dirt and glass shards from the attack, but the more I thought about it, it was probably best the wound wasn't cleaned until we got to the CSH unit. The powerlessness I felt was unreal. To know better about how to care for a wound than the emergency room staff, yet be unable to help, to have to entrust myself to people whose ultimate motives I didn't know . . . I learned things about faith in those moments I had never had to learn before.

Above all, I was trying to stay awake. *You have got to stay with it,* I told myself. I knew that falling asleep now might be the last time I ever did so.

By now, I saw that they were really starting to focus more on David, and I thought again that it was because he was a man, and therefore, more valuable to society. But something gnawed at me, suggesting maybe he'd been hurt worse than he appeared. Then I heard him speaking, and he sounded as much like himself as ever, so I pushed away my fears. His voice was animated and distinctly David.

There was an Iraqi policeman standing nearby and I asked in my broken Arabic, "American soldiers?"

He nodded and said, "They are coming."

David asked again, in his better Arabic, "American soldiers coming?"

Again, we were assured they were on their way. I wonder how much time had actually passed since the attack. It seemed like we'd spent days getting to the hospital, and we still weren't in the right hands.

I remember fighting to stay awake, saying to the doctor, "Lady doctor, help me." She just nodded in reply.

I did have a sense that I was all right, meaning that I was going to survive, but the wait for the American soldiers seemed interminable. I knew the base wasn't far—*Where were they?* At this point, I didn't know how long I could stay awake, and I needed to know they'd be there before I allowed myself to yield to the weight of fatigue that was trying to close my eyes.

When the American soldiers finally came, relief flooded me, but it was short-lived. "We're not medics," one of them said immediately. "We're here to protect you until the medics arrive." My joy faltered, but I have to say their presence did so much for me mentally.

A soldier, whom I remember only as Tim, came to me and said, "You've got to stay focused on me." He was tall, and I'll tell you, there is nothing like the sight of an American soldier in battle gear to allay one's fears in a threatening situation. I was so glad to be in the presence of my countryman, so thankful to have my citizenship. Just his standing guard reminded me the medics were on their way, and I knew David and I had the protection we needed. It may sound odd, but they provided a sense of normalcy for us. If we'd been home and called 911, it would have provided the same sense of relief that someone was in charge. Contrary to my uncertainty about the people at the hospital, I knew these soldiers wanted us to survive and would do everything in their power to make it happen.

By now, I'd lost a lot of blood, and I wanted to sleep so badly. The soldiers comforted me as if they were my own angels sent to sing for me. I asked Tim if he was a believer in Jesus, and I guess I should have been surprised that he said yes, but for some reason, I wasn't.

"Pray for me?" I said.

Tim nodded and called another soldier over to us. I believe his name was Chad, but my memory is hazy. Chad got on his knees at the head of my bed, and he prayed. He prayed thoroughly for David and me, and comfort enveloped me. This soldier, praying for us in the heart of an Iraqi hospital, with his gun at the ready, meant so much to me. Everything felt so foreign, but this felt natural. This felt like a warm blanket.

Then there was David's voice, still talking and still strong, giving me comfort. It was as it should have been. David was still in charge and I trusted he would handle everything like he always did. Once when David was with a mission team in Africa, his fellow teammates told him he talked too much. They laid hands on him and prayed over him. If I had been there I would have told them to save their breath! David was an energetic, extroverted, gregarious, never-met-a-stranger leader. That's who God made him to be. He was always the journalist he trained to be, narrating every situation as though cementing it in his mind for eternity. I loved the sound of his voice, and he *never* spoke too much for me. He was the man who never missed anything in his surroundings, and it was no different in the midst of the Iraqi hospital as he relayed everything he'd seen to the Iraqi police and the American soldiers.

David told them what had happened in full detail, as he'd done on countless videos in the Sudan and in his many journals. David saw life with the detail of an artist, and he left nothing out as he went on describing what had happened. I didn't focus on what he was saying, only the reassuring sound of his voice. I could hear the doctors speaking to each other, and I realized they were very concerned about David now. The doctors spoke in Arabic, but I couldn't understand the medical terms. I wished now I had listened more closely to my nurse mother, an operating room RN, when she talked of medical conditions.

One of the surgeons spoke directly to me, and I struggled to understand. I finally heard the word "tube" in the tangle of Arabic words. "Tube?" They nodded. Looking back, I think they must have wanted to put some kind of drainage tube in David's chest. At the time I only knew they were concerned, David needed a tube, and I was in no position to argue. I longed to touch David, to hold his hand and let him know we were together in this. Even if I could have reached out to him, it wouldn't have been appropriate in the Muslim world.

"How long until the medics get here?" I asked the soldiers, nervous over the Iraqi doctor's request to take action on David.

"Five minutes."

"Can he wait five minutes?" I asked the doctor, unwilling for them to operate if there was any chance the military medics would be arriving soon.

"Yes," they answered together after conferring. But as the minutes ticked on, I could see the concern in their faces. Five minutes was stretching into ten, and David's condition was worsening.

Where are the helicopters?

I later found out the helicopters were being shot at and were unable to land. The Army had to diffuse the situation before they could put the helicopters on the ground and transport us to the CSH unit.

"We need to do something," the Iraqi doctor said urgently, referring to David. Without the American medics, we had no choice.

I nodded. "If he needs help now, then you do it, but when the medics get here, he gets handed over to the Americans," I said in Arabic.

The doctors agreed. "This is your husband?" they asked, clarifying that I had the right to make decisions.

"Yes, he is," I said.

As soon as David's gurney turned the hallway corner for surgery, the soldiers received word that the helicopter had landed. I never heard their rotors, never had an inkling of their arrival until the soldiers spoke. But just knowing they were there gave me another infusion of peace. I so wanted to sleep.

Tim, my guardian-angel soldier, looked at me. "Keep talking to me," he said. "Where are you from?" He was obviously trying to keep me awake.

I didn't want to talk anymore. Every breath was becoming a struggle. My chest felt as though I had an army tank parked on it. Trying to fill my lungs with air felt impossible. My vision was fuzzy and the soldier's face wavered in front of me. I didn't want to talk anymore. I just wanted to sleep.

"If you don't want to talk," Tim said, startling me, "you keep your eyes on me." He told me he was from North Carolina and continued to ramble, while I just stared into his eyes, willing myself to keep my eyes opened. *David needs me*, I thought. The time finally came to be transported to the CSH unit. "Okay, we have to take you outside," Tim said.

As we got outside, the whirring of the rotors sounded like a steady heartbeat. It was dark now, and I could feel the cold seeping into my open thigh, the reedy grass slicing against me in the wind. The helicopter's rotors kicked up dust, and I worried it would get into my cuts. My instinct was to cover myself, but my arms were paralyzed. David and I were on the helipad together, and I wanted so badly to help him as much as he wanted to help me.

Tim looked at me one final time, and said, "Okay, they've got you now." The medics positioned me on the helicopter, the gurney bouncing uncomfortably, and I was strapped in place.

"Are you going with me?" I asked, trying hard to be heard over the roar of the helicopter's motors. I would miss Tim's strength and calm nature. I didn't want him to go. He'd been such a comfort, and I would miss knowing a fellow believer was there with me, praying while David and I focused on what lay ahead. I was giving up the only sense of peace I knew at the time, and it scared me.

"No, I can't go," Tim shouted. "But they've got you now."

I was starting to feel more pain, and I was barely aware of my surroundings once on the helicopter. I knew I was in the air, probably in further danger, but none of that bothered me as we fluttered along to the CSH unit. I only thought of this as the last stop on our journey towards help and safety at the American hospital. The flight wasn't long, and as I felt the helicopter touch ground, I breathed a deep sigh of relief. When I was pulled off the helicopter I realized David wasn't on the chopper with me. I was assured there were two helicopters, and he'd be arriving soon. Once again, I started to worry and had a renewed spirit to stay awake. I had to know he was with me, and that he'd made it.

They put me on a stretcher and wheeled me into the clean room, to prepare me for surgery. What a stark contrast the sixty-seventh

CSH unit was from the Iraqi hospital! Although the tent was Army-green camouflage and rustic, the latest medical equipment lined the walls, and I felt as though I was finally in America. Surgeons acted with the skill and grace of any big American city trauma unit, and I relaxed at the thought that I didn't have to worry anymore. *Praise God.*

I heard David arrive at the door, and I felt my heart speed at his arrival. I heard him pray, "Jesus, we don't know what's happening. Just help us." As they wheeled him in, he hollered across the hospital, "I love you!" in his loud, booming voice. I smiled with tears in my eyes at the sound of his familiar shout.

And I yelled back, "I love you, too!"

"We're gonna make it through this, baby!" David called.

"Okay," I shouted back weakly. I remember the questioning faces over me. "That's my husband," I said through my tears. "He's a good man. You take care of him." I kept repeating the words, over and over. "He's a good man. You take care of him."

"Okay, we will, but we've got to look at you now."

I had my left leg propped up, and it throbbed. It had been nearly blown off by a bullet just below the knee, and its bent position was the most comfortable. The doctors said they were going to stretch out my leg now, and I braced for it, anticipating what I'd felt when exiting the truck earlier. I wanted it bent and I knew straightening it meant more pain, excruciating pain.

"On the count of three," the doctor warned. They pushed my bent leg towards the table, and I felt my bones in places so unnatural. I still cringe thinking about the pain. But I barely cried out. My entire body was racked with pain, but the leg straightened. And I remained stoic throughout.

The doctor told me he'd seen tough soldiers scream out louder than that, and I smiled at my brief display of strength. I think I'd only been trying to make up for my moment of screaming into the ears of the Arab men who helped me on the street.

An older doctor was checking out the damage to my face and nose. His features were peaceful to me, calming just by his demeanor. "You're going to be all right. We're going to fix you up. You'll be fine."

These doctors saw horrific battle wounds everyday, and I knew they could take care of me, but I'll never forget that doctor's face or his sense of composure and what it did for me. He, more than any of the others, gave me a sense that this wasn't the end. I would indeed survive.

At that moment, I just remember praying to the Lord, "Thank you. Thank you."

"We have to prep you for surgery," I heard someone say. "We're going to have to take out your earrings."

I had these little wire heart earrings that David had given me. They were extremely difficult to get out, to the point that I generally just wore them all the time rather than go through the trouble of removing them. A guy in the unit worked forever to get the first earring out, while I stared at the green draped tent ceiling. After a long battle with the tiny loop wire, he started on the second one and I thought, *We are never going to get me into surgery at this rate.* I remember looking at him wrestling with an earring in the midst of a room full of state of the art, high-tech medical equipment. I couldn't believe a tiny earring was causing such a delay.

"Should we get a *girl* to take these out?" I said, and I heard laughter in the room. I was proud of myself for disarming a tense situation with a bit of humor since that was usually David's job.

During all the prep work I could hear David talking and his voice soothed me. David loved to talk, and his voice brought me comfort and a sense of normalcy. But even in that comfort I could hear his voice getting weaker. I knew he was in the right place, and that he was getting the help he needed. But as his wife, I wanted to reach across to the next bed. It was so hard not being able to comfort him, to hold his hand and soothe him and just be there for him as the helpmate I promised to be. I was thankful to be beside him, but to be powerless to hold his hand felt like torture.

David reiterated what he'd seen for another set of inquiring soldiers. He was the only one in the car who could really speak to that, and he detailed all he'd seen while I listened, pacified by his voice. It wasn't the words—I can't tell you what he said. It was just his warm baritone giving the small details, as he'd learned to do in his journals. David saw the world in detail, and in the midst of the attack he could have written the entire thing from a journalist's point of view. Because of his former profession, he was uniquely gifted for that task.

"How's my husband?" I asked one of the doctors.

They could see I was agitated about David's condition, and one of the doctors left my side to converse with David's doctors while I waited.

"He'll survive," the doctor came back and told me.

I just remember feeling so tired then, as if, finally, I could rest. David would survive. I was determined to be there with him. One of the nurses prepping me for surgery seemed surprised to see my eyes still open. "Is it okay for me to sleep now?" I asked her.

She said yes, and I closed my eyes to the camouflage-draped ceiling. I woke up in Dallas, Texas—eight days later.

* * *

"Clearly there has been a shift in the insurgency and the way the extremists are conducting operations," said Lt. Gen. Ricardo Sanchez, ranking American commander in Iraq, March 16, 2004.

CHAPTER THREE

A Shared Desire for Iraq

David—1999

Iraq wasn't our first visit into a country ravaged by war. On the contrary, David and I had been stationed in countries known for their violence, from Israel's constant battle with the Palestinians to the unrest and genocide in the Sudan. Our road into Iraq was a long one, fraught with everyday dangers that became commonplace.

Journeyman is a two-year program that allows college graduates to get a taste of foreign humanitarian field work without making a long-term commitment. Assignments are given based on a person's expressed interest in a people group, combined with his or her talents and education.

In the Journeyman library there are stacks of resources detailing the needs in various countries and mission fields. David McDonnall, newly graduated from West Texas A&M University, and rife with anticipation to serve, started his assignment as a researcher for remote areas in 1999. Basically, his job was to pave the way for Christian relief workers to establish humanitarian services in lands where none existed. It was a Lawrence of Arabia-type job for the relief sector, filled with adventure and unknowns. It was perfect for David, who loved venturing into unfamiliar territory and seeing places and people groups most people won't even read about in a newspaper.

David prayed and sensed a call into the Arab world. His call was not out of knowledge—David was totally unfamiliar with the Arab world. This was the area God laid on his heart, so he headed to Jordan to learn Arabic. His focus would ultimately be on the Sudan and North Africa. His job description was to find and research the different people groups living in northern Sudan and assess their needs for a better life: water, housing, food, and other basic necessities.

Sudan is the largest country in Africa, and because its history is so violent, relief workers are in limited supply. Not many are willing to enter a country where genocide has been the standard operating procedure of the leadership.

Before going to Africa, David needed to learn Arabic and get comfortable living in an Arab culture. Arriving in Jordan in March, he found his language school didn't begin until the fall. Therefore, he began "learning by immersion"—throwing himself into the culture, learning everything he could. That was like throwing Brer Rabbit into the briar patch—nothing pleased David more.

When he arrived in Jordan he was like a puppy whose tail won't stop wagging. He couldn't wait to get started, to explore Jordan, to learn to depend on God completely, to learn the power of prayer and the majesty of God. He wrote in his journal, "In order to live out what I plan, I must die to self. I must crucify my will to allow the Holy Spirit to control my life." It wasn't that David was blinded or without fear, for he also wrote, "A look at a verse often touted— Mark 10:29–31. It says anyone who has left homes or family for the sake of Christ will receive one hundred times more in this age. Yet, if you keep reading, it says in verse 30 that while you will receive many blessings, you will receive persecutions, also. Persecutions are counted in the blessings we receive. *Oh God, help me to see persecutions as a blessing.*"

Although David had prayed about and had a heart for Arab Muslims, he wasn't exactly sure who they were. He learned that Arab and Muslim are not interchangeable terms. Arab is a racial or ethnic term, and Muslim is a religious term. There are some Arabs who are Christians, which surprised him, though the vast majority are obviously Muslim. It sounds basic, but for a country boy from Colorado, it was the first light bulb moment of many to come.

He called his Jordanian apartment "the Palace." It had marble floors, a living room with satellite TV, and three large bedrooms. It also had a massive balcony that overlooked the city, complete with a built-in barbeque grill. To someone used to living at the poverty level in college, it was magnificent. He would share the apartment with six other workers on the team who were learning English and Arabic in differing stages of their own training for service in Sudan. The young men became each other's family. The team leader was like their father away from home.

The food was definitely to David's liking. He loved to eat, and he often described a meal with the full intensity of a gourmet. His first foray into Arab food was hummus with flat bread and lamb and rice. And while he enjoyed the meal, he was thrilled when they went into a westernized section of Amman, Jordan, and saw Arby's, Blimpie's, Dunkin' Donuts and even a Hard Rock Café. *This was living the missionary life?* David felt like a king.

Of course, all that glitters is not gold, and although the women were wearing jeans and T-shirts in the more westernized parts of the country, there were other sections of Jordanian towns where homes had barred windows—not to keep intruders out, but to keep the women inside.

Besides the spacious accommodations and food, the biggest bonus that appealed to David's extroverted personality was that every event in the Arab culture is a social one. From shopping in the marketplace to purchasing gas, one does not plan any meeting or lesson without including time for a visit. It was a lifestyle that appealed to David and his love of all things social. He could strike up a conversation with anyone, and the Arab people would respond. The Arab culture is very much like the way North Americans view Latin American cultures: overflowing with friendly hospitality and great food, coffee, and tea.

Even with all the "luxuries," David was still homesick. After being there less than a week, he wrote in his journal, "Right now I'm extremely happy to hear cussing. I know that sounds strange coming from a Christian worker, but let me explain. Brad [his roommate] and I found the Arnold Schwarzenegger film, *Eraser*, on TV. We were watching the opening credits, and we were praying the movie would be in English. Even with satellite TV, it's an unexpected rarity to find anything, let alone an Arnold Schwarzenegger movie, in English. So hearing Arnold cuss in English brought a bit of joy. But our excitement was short-lived. Five minutes into the movie, the transmission went out."

The television satellite was a global feed, so they received programming from Russia, Syria, Egypt, Algeria, and Jordan. Rarely did something from the United States ever appear on their TV. The good news was it forced the men to work on their Arabic skills. Life definitely took more effort in David's palace. Even a simple shower was a challenge. The hot water in his luxurious apartment didn't work so he took his leader's advice and heated two kettles of water and poured them into a big pan. After ten minutes of heating water he would head to the shower with a large pan and a mug to provide the "shower" aspect. He poured the water over him with the mug and discovered that a shower was a forty-minute procedure. He later said he would never again take something as simple as hot water for granted.

After his first Jordanian shower, David went to tour another part of downtown Amman and ended up at the Roman amphitheater. He could almost hear the roar of the lions and the throngs that once gathered there to watch Christians be persecuted by soldiers. It was a visual reminder of what his spiritual predecessors had endured to preach the Word of Christ.

As he found his bearings in the Middle East, David settled down to learn the language and how to communicate in Arabic. One thing that helped in this regard is that people feel completely comfortable talking about religion. In America it's such a taboo subject, but in this world where there are so many different religions living in the same small area, people are interested in discussing it and desire to understand the differences.

Once at a birthday party for a fellow team worker, David was introduced to three young Sudanese men. Of course, he was more than anxious to learn about the country that was his ultimate destination. The men were students at a Jordanian Christian seminary, and David listened with rapt attention as they told him how the Sudanese treat visitors with great honor and hospitality. Demographically, northern Sudan was historically Christian, but because there were no Bibles in their language, when Islam swept the area many of the Sudanese were swept up into the new religion. However, the people of northern Sudan still followed many Christian traditions.

At the same party, David also talked to another young Sudanese student from the Nuba Mountains in Sudan, a primarily Muslim stronghold. David learned how the man had been persecuted, including stoning and imprisonment, for preaching the gospel. When David asked him why he planned to return to a country where he'd endured such hardship, the student looked at him and said in a polite and humble voice, "Oh yes, Sudan is the only place for me."

Many of the Nuba Mountain people are Muslim extremists who will stop at nothing to promote Islam. Unlike the "borderline" Muslims in the north, millions of Nuba Mountain people are fanatic supporters of radical Islam. This young seminary student told David that change was taking place "primarily because Christians around the world are praying for the Sudan. Any time before God moves in an area, lots of prayer is essential."

David lit up with enthusiasm from his first contact with a Sudanese group of men. He saw how great the need was, and he wanted to get started. He wrote, "Those who have suffered hardships to pull the rocks in these areas are now being rewarded. The blood of these martyrs is watering the harvest fields of today."

Later that week, David praised God in a worship service held by Sudanese believers and listened for the first time to Christian believers praising God in Arabic. While the call to Muslim prayer went out over the city, he felt another world inside the confines of the church. He prayed for those in the Sudan to experience the same satisfaction in God that he enjoyed, "for one day, all will glorify God!"

David always enjoyed his independence. He was content to be in the mountains of Colorado with only the quiet to keep him company, so although he was very extroverted, he wasn't quite as social as the Arab culture—yet. David endured culture shock with the close-knit ways of the families in the Middle East. Extended families all live together in the same building—if not the same house. A father will build his home, and when his own son is ready to take a wife, he'll often add a floor to the house to accommodate his son and the son's new wife. This happens throughout the generations, and to an American who might be expected to leave the family home at eighteen or so, it felt claustrophobic at first.

David's language teacher and her extended family became good friends and mentors as he assimilated into the culture. Abraham* was a young man in Jordan who was deeply rooted in the group known as Shabaab—Arabic for "young men." Although there were clear divisions between the sexes, teens generally did the same things in Jordan as in America, such as hanging out, drinking tea, and even cruising the city streets in cars. The longer he lived in Jordan, the more Arab David became.

Lee*, an American who lived in Jordan with his family, oversaw the men in David's apartment and their quest to learn the Arabic culture and language. He was David's mentor and was a man committed to "raising his boys up in the way they should go." With weekly meetings, David learned from Lee what it meant to be a Christian relief worker in a Muslim country. This is the man who would eventually marry us; David looked up to him like no other on this earth.

Once, when Lee came for a visit to the apartment, he remarked to the roommates, "I admire you guys and your dedication to your work—especially the lengths you go to prepare yourself for living in the bush and 'hole' motels. Your bathroom is certainly as bad, if not worse, than most bathrooms in the Sudan. Way to go, guys!"

Since there was no plumbing to speak of in the Sudan, David went straight to work cleaning the bathrooms. He strove to be a man above reproach, and hearing that his bathroom represented a Third World country was not the image he was striving for. He continued to pour himself into Bible study and listened for God's voice while he learned Arabic and the ways of the culture.

On one of his first hospitality experiences in Jordan, he'd taken a trip with the new journeymen to a crusader-era castle, which was a main tourist site in the country. While there he met some Arab men who told him they were having a wedding feast and celebration in their village and wanted David and his fellow journeymen to join them. In America, such an invitation from complete strangers would seem odd. But David was learning that in the Arab world, they wanted to share their joy with everyone. That was part of the celebration.

David and his team feasted like kings at the wedding party and watched as the men in the village square gathered to dance, so that the entire village could watch from the hills. He found a new love for the Arab culture in that wedding because he wasn't just a bystander—he was a participant. His earlier feelings of claustrophobia began to dissipate.

Once David's training began, Jordan would serve as the home base for trips to the Sudan. His new schedule consisted of two months in the Sudan and a month back in Jordan to rest and debrief and write up papers about all he'd seen in the Sudan. Notes were very important, and David's journalism background served him well. The team encountered some people groups that had never been visited by Caucasians. In order to provide relief efforts to the region, meticulous notes and location coordinates were recorded for teams that would follow. David's life was starting to reflect the adventure he'd sought. He wrote this in his journal after being on the training circuit for a year:

"I studied Arabic, spent the weekend at a wild wedding party in a Jordanian village, climbed in the pyramids and the Sphinx, survived a major earthquake in Istanbul [which he slept through], learned to dive and did so in the Red Sea, rode a ferry across the Nile with a boat full of camels and donkeys, walked the Via de la Rosa on Good Friday, visited all the major sites of Jesus' life and ministry, crossed under the Suez Canal, camped in the northern Sudanese desert, met a former NBA player, as well as a high school friend in Khartoum, Sudan, ate at a wild seafood restaurant in Cyprus, ate five loaves and two fish at the shores of the Sea of Galilee, saw the 'treasury' of Indiana Jones' fame at Petra . . . ."

And he wrote all of the above from the Cairo airport. David McDonnall lived life to the full, and he was most fulfilled doing the Lord's work in nations that most of us will never see.

CHAPTER FOUR

My Life in Israel

Carrie—1999

While David created a life in Jordan and the Sudan, I, not knowing David or his work, started my own Journeyman time in an Israeli-Arab village in Israel. I worked in a foster home for Arab children, cleaning the bathrooms, scrubbing the floors, and sometimes helping the cook on special *falafel* nights. The world I entered was completely foreign to me as well. On my entrance into Israel, I learned that my nickname sounded remarkably like a curse word in Arabic, so I had to go by my formal name, Carrie. Not only was I learning a new language and culture, but I felt like an undercover agent, as I had to get used to a new identity as well.

It was ridiculous to whine over a name change, but life was so foreign to me when I arrived: the food, the language, the culture—even the introduction of menial labor after graduating college was new. The last thing I needed was a new name. *Well*, I reasoned, *God changed Sarai's name and Jacob's and a myriad of other great people. Who am I to protest?*

Arriving in Israel was a mixed blessing for me. Dayton, my nephew-to-be, was making his way into the world, and as I rejoiced in his new life, and all the possibilities that lay ahead for him, I struggled with my own self-worth. "Why?" I wrote in my journal. "This event triggered questions I thought I had figured out. I am a nobody in the big scheme of things; I am a peon. So with this as a basic fact, what use am I to God? What or how much glory can we really give from this life? Is my scrubbing toilets really giving praise to His name? I miss my family, my home, and my life. I am here, Lord, where You have brought me, so what are You going to do?"

I watched as Arab children in the area were treated poorly, and I instantly felt a connection towards them. The longstanding conflict between Israelis and Palestinians created a harsh environment, especially for those children without two parents. The foster home I worked in provided food, clothing, and education until the Arab children were eighteen. And although the parents were alive, the foster care system worked more like an orphanage. The children lived and learned at the home and prepared for their futures while their parents sorted out their own difficulties. Most of the parents didn't have authority over their children, much as if Child Protective Services were to take them away in America. Either the living conditions in their homes were unacceptable or their parents were unfit or otherwise incapable of raising them.

The foster home where I served was built like a normal family building, offering different floors for separate branches of the family. The family who ran the foster home lived on the ground floor—the main living area of the house. Beneath the main floor were a bomb shelter and a basement area where the kitchen, dining room, and laundry area for the children was located. Additionally, a young family, the maintenance worker and his wife (the maid) and two children, lived on this floor.

I was told the husband in that family, a "jack of all trades, master of none," knew English and would help me with Arabic. I discovered that the extent of his English was "hello"—not a great start in acquiring language skills. The first Arabic word I learned was "throw" because my first job was to sort through old clothes given to the orphanage.

The floor where the boys lived—between the main floor and the basement—had a central area with desks for instruction and surrounding rooms with bunks for sleeping. Above the main floor was a similar floor for girls. This made for a lot of bathrooms, all of which had to be cleaned every day. All told, there were thirty to forty children living there, depending on the day.

The children brought light into the home and my world. Most of them were from poverty-stricken families, and I quickly learned not to ask too much about their home life. It was a source of pain for most of them. Their dark brown eyes would usually focus on the ground as they quietly answered such questions.

The kids loved hugs, especially the younger ones. I never turned them away from a hug, unless I saw them scratching their heads—a telltale sign of lice in the Middle East. I never had lice at home, but I fought it my entire two years in Israel. My mother would send me lice care packages, as the lice in Israel had mutated beyond what the local drug store treatments could handle.

In the big courtyard outside the home, cars would be moved from the driveway, and a small soccer field would take shape. I could hear the sounds of courtyard tag, basketball, soccer, and sing-song games, and I was always aware that a ball might be coming in my direction at any time. I loved to hear the constant chatter of the children and the sounds of playfulness in their voices. Seeing them laugh made me laugh and brought joy to my heart. I got to know them intimately through the games that were held on the hill above my "apartment."

It wasn't an easy life, but I knew I was appreciated. I played the guitar in the sanctity of my room while lamenting the lack of spicy Texas food. And I grew very attached to the home and the plight of the children. In the quiet of my room I would listen to praise music and marvel at the biblical-looking village in which I lived. Being near where my Savior walked felt miraculous every day.

Speaking of my room—during my two-year stay in Israel, I lived in a converted metal shipping container. I remember when I saw it I thought, *You have got to be kidding me! This is what my supervisors were calling an apartment? How long had it been since they'd actually seen a legitimate apartment?* The forty-foot-by-eight-foot bin—think of the giant shipping containers that are off-loaded from ships at ports around the world—had been separated by thin pieces of plywood into three apartments with separate bathrooms. The orphanage owner had cut windows in the sides to allow a bit of air into the rooms. I tried to keep my face from showing what I truly felt the first time I saw it: dread. I gave myself pep talks and ignored my supervisor's wife's attempts at positive comments. After all, she lived in a two-story house.

The owner of the foster home showed my apartment to me like it was the hottest piece of real estate in the area. I didn't want to hurt his feelings, but I was apprehensive when I saw the mold growing on the walls and no sink (though one was promised). Mentally, I went through what my life would be like: I'd be spitting in the toilet and rinsing my toothbrush and washing my hands in the shower.

Undaunted by my reaction, the owner turned on the window unit that jutted from the wall, proudly demonstrating how it worked. My container was freezing in the winter, scorching in the summer, and I had regular visits by slugs—but never the cockroaches my neighbors complained about. (Although with only plywood to separate us, one could never be sure.)

Fortunately, I had a few days to adjust to the idea of living in a giant shipping container before it became my home for the following two years. I had such fun telling my Journeyman friends about my new home. We laughed when I told them of my supervisor's attempts to pretty it up by calling it an apartment.

"It's a shipping container!" I said. "I'm going to live in a shipping container! And not even a whole shipping container—one-third of it."

My friends would tease me when I would visit, occasionally pointing out other "containers" along the roadside. "Oh, it looks like they forgot to call and tell you they're moving you!" they'd say and laugh, followed by, "Oh look! That one looks like a double-wide. I bet you could trade up!"

I measured my container room once, and it was eight feet by eleven feet. It was not exactly better than your average jail cell, nor more luxurious. I did have a phone in the room, but couldn't dial out on it. Basically, it was a glorified intercom system. I knew my phone calls could be monitored, and therefore my complaining was saved for God alone. I tried to be sensible, to tell myself, *This is where you are called to be.* Or, *You'll get used to it in time.*

God had some weeding and pruning to do in the garden that was my life, but I can't say I was looking forward to it. The heart of Mother Teresa had yet to prosper within me. Those were the first days of ministry for me, and I had a lot to learn. One saving grace was that I had Internet access in my room, though I was warned it would be "sluggish." That didn't sound good, but access to the Internet beckoned like a jail break after realizing my apartment was an extra-large tin can with a view.

However, this was my first international mission experience, and I viewed it as part of the ambience necessary for my deep spiritual growth. It was that way until I met David and got a glimpse of his apartment, luxurious by comparison.

Amazingly enough, my container did start to feel like home. I spruced it up as best I could. I was given a copy of the Mona Lisa, which I placed right outside my bathroom—just like Daddy Warbucks from *Annie*. It only seemed right. I lined the ceiling with lights my first Christmas and left them up year-round. Then, I added pictures to my wall that I had taken from my favorite spots in Israel: the Sea of Galilee, the Mount of Olives, and the Eastern Wall of the Temple Mount. I covered the doors of my armoire with pictures from college and my Aggie history at Texas A&M: the Bonfire, the Elephant Walk, my best friend from college, and the Aggie Ring Dance. I also had a family wall that included pictures of my mom and dad, my sister, and her kids. Later, I would add pictures of my "new" family, an adopted family in Israel. I also had pictures and cards the children had drawn for me. By the time I left, my collage told a story of how much my life had changed—actually, how much *I* had changed.

It's amazing how you can be more consistent in the Bible and spiritual disciplines without the world's distractions. Living in a small village, I realized how much I could live without and how much I enjoyed it. Just the absence of city noise was a new blessing, since I'd never lived on a quiet village street. Because they were built before the advent of cars, some of the village streets were only accessible by carts and bicycles.

Stripped of so many things—my nickname, formal living quarters, a familiar language, friends, family—I had to look to the Lord. I made a point to have my quiet time each morning after my chores. I set myself a rule: I could not practice my guitar, dulcimer, or check e-mail (which became a real motivator after I met David!) until I'd had my prayer time. I learned to rely upon God and not myself.

The children weren't allowed to play by my container, but they would often sneak down and come knocking. Sometimes they'd just knock politely and ask if I could play. Other times the kids would climb on top of the container and begin drumming on my roof. Their favorite game with the container was to drumbeat the sides of it in the same fashion of a skilled *dorbecky* (Mideast drum) player.

I was learning to play the guitar and the hammer dulcimer. With the absence of television I was amazed at how much more free time I had. I would sit outside on my "porch" on beautiful days and practice my instruments. The kids would gather around me and listen. Sometimes I let them try, and then I would play them a tune. A few danced and added their own silly words to the song, and they'd be caught up in the moment. Once the play-yard monitor would notice them missing, he or she would call them back up to the field.

Sometimes the girls living in the home would want to come into my apartment. The owner of the home advised against it (sadly, he was afraid they'd steal), but if there were two of them, I would allow it, and I would show them pictures of my family and let them play my instruments. At other times, I would join the girls in their quarters and drink hot tea, watch TV, and we'd dance together, laughing the entire time.

One group of siblings at the home particularly touched me. There were four children, two girls and two boys. Their mother would faithfully visit them each week, and they would run into her open arms and then rummage through the bag of homemade goodies she'd brought. She was a kind woman, but just couldn't support her four children. I don't believe there was a husband around, so rather than let her kids roam the streets, she put them in the care of the home. In the meantime, she was working hard to save money to get them back with her. She even sacrificed riding the bus, which cost just a few *shekels,* choosing to walk from her neighboring village instead. Watching this made you thankful for the American welfare system which provides a safety net for mothers like this.

The woman's eldest daughter, Jamiila*, was very proficient in her conversational English, considering she rarely had opportunity to use it. I would usually look to her to get a definition of a word I didn't understand or to learn one I needed to complete my thought. The family was so special to me, and there was talk they would actually be able to go home soon after I left. Their eyes lit up at the thought. Early in my stay, when my language skills were sorely lacking, I went to the grocery store to get trash bags. When I returned home I found I had purchased lunch sacks. So I came to rely more and more on Jamiila and her translations.

There were so many sights in Israel that were worth a second look. I really loved seeing how random some of the city sights were. I saw an entire family living in a bomb shelter, a camel in the front seat of a car, goats in vehicles, and a Depend undergarment taped to a shop window as an advertisement. There was just so much to take in as I absorbed this new culture.

I loved my work there, as menial as it was. I loved being around the children and also being in the international community. The village, located in the hills of Israel, was picturesque. I had a lovely view of the lush, rolling landscape, and the neighboring buildings around me. The green, flourishing trees and the hills reminded me every day, "I lift my eyes to the hills . . . ."

Because the foster home sat on the side of a hill, and my room was on a flat part, I looked up at the beautiful landscape that enveloped me. My host family would even invite me into their kitchen for the morning which, on a clear day, offered a far-away view of the crystal Mediterranean Sea. The town smelled divine as I was right across the street from an Arab coffee-roasting company. I woke up every morning to the heavenly scent of the rich brew. In the evening we were offered spectacular sunsets on the horizon.

The village had all the familiar elements of an American city—a grocery store, an elementary school, a post office—but I didn't like walking around the city by myself. It was still foreign with a different language, and being the lone blonde in the region made me stand out. I was used to being an extrovert and very social, but I soon found that I did not like being stared at. The negative attention—being stared at for being a female—grew tiresome, and I learned to tone down my appearance when I would walk in the village.

Since my duties were limited at the foster home, I found another purpose in meeting with the Arab families in the region and getting to know them. Realizing I was so far from home, one family in particular took me in and treated me as their daughter. They were a Muslim family, and I grew very attached to their daughter, Jane*.

At the end of the work day I would walk over and meet Jane, and we would just hang out or make cookies. Her home gave me a place to go, so I felt like I had family in the area. She became one of my closest friends in Israel; I loved her family like my own and I miss her like a sister. I learned to make an Arabic cookie from her family, and how to insert the fig into the dough (easier than it looks) and bake them in an old-fashioned oven. This family took me everywhere with them and provided a sense of fitting in, in a place where I clearly didn't. The hospitality of this family, and others I met, was something I came to treasure.

The curfew in the Arab village took some getting used to. It just wouldn't look proper for a woman to be out after dark on the streets, so I set my internal clock to be home by the time the sun went down. Since I had to rise early for work, it wasn't a huge sacrifice—just an adjustment I made to serve the Lord.

One day my friend Jane came and picked me up. It was Saturday—*shabbat*—so most everyone had the day off. Her family had planned to picnic in the countryside, so she came with her brothers, her sister-in-law, her niece, and her mother. With me, our number totaled six-and-a-half, in a car that seated five.

We crammed into the car, the trunk loaded down with the picnic food, and traveled north, traversing the hills and the thin road cut for donkey carts, not cars. We passed many other picnickers as we drove. It was a great day to be outside. Spring was in full bloom in Israel, and everyone wanted to enjoy it. We soon left civilization and entered into a field that did not have a road.

Jane explained that this field was the site of her great grandfather's house and village. We would picnic among the ruins. As we rolled to a stop I saw that Jane's grandmother, her aunt, and youngest brother were there, along with one of his friends. Her grandmother looked ancient, far beyond her actual years, but in her eyes there was the sparkle of youth. I loved Jane's grandmother. When she greeted me, I was no less than royalty to her. These greetings were always elaborate and welcoming, even if I'd just seen her a few days earlier. Her thick accent was always hard for me to decipher with my limited Arabic. However, her smiles and kisses were universal, and I knew I was always welcome in her family and her home.

On the picnic grounds, Auntie was busy spreading a blanket. Our car's occupants were greeted with the traditional "*Sallaam alekum*," ("Hello, how are you?" but literally, "Peace be upon you all") and we each offered our response, "*Wa alekum isalaam*" ("And peace be upon you"). I was soon greeted again with "*Ahlan, ya Kaarie* ("Hello, Carrie;" my name with a thick Arabic accent), "*keef halik Kaarie?*" ("How are you?"). I never quite understood why they were so eager not only to accept me, but to go out of their way to do so.

I began to help unload the food but was soon asked to sit still and just be a guest. Jane's oldest brother soon had a fire started to grill some chicken pieces and other meats. Fresh vegetables were being cut and the hummus uncovered and set out as a dip. As the food was being prepared everyone began asking how I was and how my life was at the home. Had I talked with my parents and were they doing well? This afforded me a good opportunity to practice my Arabic. I must confess that I often cheated, as I allowed Jane to translate the harder sentences for me.

Soon the meal was ready and we all gathered on the blanket—no need for plates or forks and knives. The salads we divided into a few bowls and set around the blanket in arm's reach of everyone who was eating. Everyone had a spoon and ate from the same bowl, keeping to one side of the bowl. As I was a guest, they would insist that I have my own bowl. I would argue but knew it was futile. Everything else was set in front of us. You just took what you wanted with your hands, often using a small piece of pita bread as your spoon: pinch a tomato and slide it through the creamy hummus and into your mouth. Delicious!

After lunch my friend Jane and I went walking through the hillside. Off in the distance, the sun gleamed off the Sea of Galilee. I shook my head at its beauty and at my new life. As we walked, we came upon a cornerstone of what had been a house. Jane told me it had been her great-grandfather's home up until the post-World War II influx of Jewish immigrants pushed her family out of the area. It was such a visual reminder of the struggles that the land has endured.

As we walked we continued to chat about my family and life in America. I was enjoying our conversation and getting to know my new friend. Our conversation drifted naturally to deeper topics—politics, the *intifada* (Palestinian uprising), and finally spiritual questions.

"Do you pray?" she asked. "What do you pray about?"

I answered, and asked her the same questions. What a freedom to have two curious friends from different worlds collide in God's sovereignty. As our conversation continued, we grew comfortable with each other and the questions that our budding friendship allowed.

I remember turning back to laugh with her over something she'd said, and behind her lay the Sea of Galilee, shimmering as the sun's rays danced over the waters. As Jane continued to speak, I fought back tears as my thoughts faded to a time when Jesus invited men to follow Him saying, "Follow me, and I will make you fishers of men." The sight of the glistening sea served as a visual reminder of why I had come—why I got up each morning to scrub toilets. *What a privilege to share Him*, I thought, as we walked back to join her family and finish our picnic.

Although we hear so much about the strife in Israel, one thing we don't hear is how many different cultures live side by side with very little conflict. There are the Israeli-Jews, the Israeli-Arabs, the Palestinians, the Druze, and many others in this international, multi-cultural area. There is always an extreme sense of distrust between the Jews and the Arabs, but they do work and live side-by-side. Unless tensions are very high due to uprisings in the West Bank or other trouble spots, most little villages move forward every day, paying no mind to the strife.

It's not nearly as overwhelming as the television news makes it appear. If I saw in reality what CNN showed as daily life in Israel, I'd run for the nearest embassy. But life is much more mundane than that. Just think if the American networks went into America's most violent cities every day and reported on nothing but the criminal activities that took place and showed that footage every day. It would create a rather one-sided image of America. Reporters flock to the Middle East, and Gaza in particular, in pursuit of the current violence. David and I eventually became rather immune to the constant threats and warnings but grieved when the violence touched someone we knew.

Sometimes, in the safety of our homes in America, we fail to remember that every act of violence involves a person and a victim. We have dehumanized the attacks that take place, rather than remembering that God created these people as uniquely and genuinely as He did our own friends and loved ones. To look into the faces of a grieving family is no different in the Middle East than it is in America. And with so much grief to go around, my heart softened considerably during my stay in Israel. David had the same experience in Jordan and the Sudan.

After being in Israel for nearly two years, I walked to the post office one day to mail a package. An Israeli guard stopped me saying, "You can't go in there."

"Why not?" I asked, annoyed.

"Bomb squad," he replied.

I sighed. In Israel, they don't take chances. If something's left in town, they have a police team that comes in and blows it up. Sometimes it's a sack of groceries, but once in a while, it's a bomb.

The soldier pointed to the other side of town, indicating I would have to walk to the next post office in the city. Did I fear that I was within five feet of a bomb? No. By that time, I simply felt annoyance I had to go somewhere else to mail my package. That became my life in the Middle East: soldiers and guns and, in the midst of it all, children playing in the streets.

Life is more hospitable in the villages. That may sound odd with the amount of violence you hear about, but life is simply more relaxed in the small villages. People walk slowly and they take the time to greet everyone. The driving is in direct conflict to this. It's not as crazy as in Iraq but still wild. When I first arrived at the foster home, they asked if I drove, and when I replied I did, they seemed surprised. Women do drive in Israel, but it wasn't odd if a woman my age didn't. I soon learned that driving in Israel was a whole different ball game than in America.

A volunteer group came to Israel, and I wanted to take them up a particular mountain so they could get a good view. I had been there before in my car so I knew it was capable, but only if I got up enough speed to make the steep, worn, dirt incline. Once at the top, the road drops dramatically on the other side and empties onto a gravel parking area. Due to the incline, however, you can't see the road as it drops off the other side of the summit. I took three of the volunteers there, and, as I ground through the gears, I could see them getting anxious about my ability to do this. Finally, at the apex of the road, one of the men shouted, "Stop! There's no road! We're going over the side!" He unlocked the door and scrambled for the door handle.

Just before he could escape, the car lurched over the hill and landed safely in the parking area. We all had a great laugh at the man's expense. He had a military background, yet he spilled out of the car praising Jesus and searching for another, safer vehicle.

If I ever teased David about his driving, he'd be sure and bring this moment up to me, saying, "And who had someone feel it would be safer to jump from a moving vehicle rather than ride with them?"

Life in Israel took me to my knees where I met my Father. He revealed Himself to me as my provider, as the One whose only Son came to serve rather than be served. He broke my heart over the "lostness" of a beautiful culture whose people I grew to love as I love my own family. He prepared me to become a helpmate to one who was learning some of the same lessons not many miles from where I lived.

CHAPTER FIVE

When First We Met

The West Bank—New Year's Day, 2000

Our story, David's and mine together, really started on New Years' Day, 2000. My fellow Journeymen and I celebrated the millennium in the West Bank in Bethlehem, the birthplace of Jesus. It seemed like the most appropriate place to be at the beginning of the third millennium after Jesus' birth. As the sky lit up with fireworks and celebration, I thought of the date as a season of change. By contrast, my everyday shipping-container routine world made the world-level celebration I was attending feel like a dream. I wondered if I was poised to make a change, if there was a different future for me—one I hadn't anticipated.

I wondered if God had a husband for me. If He did, I prayed He would make the man's presence known to me. With all the warmth and hospitality I received in Israel, I missed the comforts of home and my own family. Loneliness was starting to rear its ugly head.

I got a message from the Holy Spirit that night: "You haven't asked." And I realized that if I did truly seek a husband, I needed to let God know exactly what I was looking for and pray that He would provide.

So, on a starry New Years' Eve, I sat down and wrote an anonymous letter to the man who would one day be my life-partner. I asked God for guidance and basically wrote myself a laundry list describing the perfect mate. I promised I would save that letter and give it to the man I would someday marry. I did just that.

The very next night, New Years' Day, Journeymen from all over the region descended upon the West Bank to celebrate the new millennium. I was introduced that night to David McDonnall who, for some reason, I spent the night calling Nathan. Since Nathan means "gift of God" I later wondered if perhaps I hadn't subliminally figured out God's answer to my prayer the night before. Consciously, I failed to make the connection and went about my evening calling this stranger Nathan.

A friend corrected me on David's real name after he left. That *faux pas* on my part was indicative of how our first meeting struck me: uneventful and inconsequential. "Ask and you shall receive" had new meaning as I looked back and discovered God's perfect timing of the answer to my prayer. He hadn't made me wait at all; I was simply blinded to the truth at that point.

Eight months later, in August of 2000, David and I met again at a Christian-sponsored basketball game in the West Bank. David was touring Israel with friends, including Chris*, whom I knew from Journeyman training. That night I learned David's real name again—and this time I remembered it. We discovered we had another mutual friend, so David wrote my name and e-mail address down to pass on to that friend. But I noted that he wrote it in his black leather address book.

I remember thinking it odd, his putting my number in such a

permanent place. Many months later he laughed, telling me he knew exactly what he was doing. When David left that evening, I can't say that our meeting left a giant impression on me. But I was genuinely intrigued and had enjoyed our time together. He lived the most interesting life, always jet-setting somewhere new. Granted, the places he went were Third World countries and his accommodations were equally humble. Still, as I continued cleaning bathrooms and scrubbing floors, and living in my shipping container, there was something intriguing about a man who could fascinate an entire Journeyman crowd with his stories.

In the summer season, our groups ran a month of sports camps for the children from all over the area. Part of the basketball game's primary focus was to allow the children to escape the strife of the nation and have a normal summer camp experience. David made me laugh, and he definitely captured my attention that August night at the basketball game. There was a spark within him that just lit up the dark sky. He was genuinely warm and friendly, he was a wonderful storyteller, and he was funny. I hoped this wasn't the last time we'd meet, and although I can't say my romantic pursuits were obvious, I didn't want this man just to walk out of my life.

When David and I ran into one another at the basketball game, one of my friends asked, "Have you known each other a long time?"

"No. We just met. Why do you ask?"

"Oh, I just noticed how comfortable you were with each other and thought you'd been friends a long time. There seemed to be something more there."

I felt pride swell up in me that someone had noticed our connection, which I was still unsure about, so I probed my friend. "What does that mean?" I asked her, secretly hoping there was something more there. My friend's teasing laughter was the only response I received.

The day following the basketball game, my friends and I drove back to the same town to meet with the people that played in the game, along with David and his friends, for dinner. Thoughts swirled in my head as I anticipated dinner that night where I'd see David again. I wanted to see if I could detect what my friend was talking about. Could I pick out any sort of spark between the two of us?

My plan that night at dinner was to strategically sit down at a table first. We were a large group with lots of tables, and I figured if he had any interest in spending time with me, he would make his way to my table and take a seat there. This is exactly what he did! Again we talked easily to one another throughout the dinner. Later, the group discussed the weekend vacation we were planning after a month of running camps.

We would spend a few days in Eilat, a beautiful coastal resort town at the top end of the Gulf of Aqaba, the northeastern arm of the Red Sea. After the camps, we more than deserved a little rest and relaxation and were anxious for the upcoming vacation. At the dinner we invited any of the others who would like to be there to join us.

David was supposed to be touring with his friend but showed some interest as we discussed our plans. He told us he hadn't seen Eilat yet but wanted to. My heart leapt to think of him going along with us, but I tried desperately not to get my hopes up. Most likely, it wouldn't happen. I'd go to Eilat, have a great time, and go back to the ministry and enjoy my life after the vacation.

David told us that, if he was going, he would catch the bus and meet us at the hostel where we would be staying in Eilat. Later he confided that he didn't want to commit then, because he wanted first to make sure it was okay with his friend, Chris*.

David told me, "I didn't want Chris to be mad at me for ditching him for some girl. Which I was . . . but I didn't want him to be mad. He wasn't."

I left that evening wondering if he would show up. As it would require a three-hour bus trip from Jordan to Eilat, I somehow doubted he would come. In my heart of hearts, I was hopeful that he would, though I fought against setting my expectations too high.

The next day my team traveled to Eilat. The whole trip down I was preoccupied with trying to make myself forget that he might be there. I tried to let myself down easy with a set of legitimate reasons why his showing up was completely impractical. All the while, I was wondering why on earth I was so preoccupied by him. It wasn't like me to be "guy-crazy" and I barely knew this man.

When we arrived at the hostel, I walked through the gates convincing myself he wouldn't show and at the same time scolding myself for caring either way. People were talking excitedly about the vacation, but I was so preoccupied I wasn't hearing a word. I looked up and, lo and behold, there he was—sitting calmly at a picnic table waiting for us to arrive. He made it seem like the most normal thing in the world for him to be there, while I was a nervous wreck.

It took a distinct effort to act casual and hide my delight at seeing him. We all checked in and threw our stuff down and headed to the boardwalk for dinner. David and I continued to stick together, in spite of being in a large group, though by now we were both getting a bit nervous. We spent a small amount of time alone watching the airplanes come and go. We didn't say anything important, but I relished that small moment in time.

The following day we all went snorkeling in the Red Sea. This was my first time, so David showed me the ropes. The group snorkeled all afternoon and then took another stroll down the boardwalk to get dinner.

As we walked and waited on the group, David asked what I would do after I finished my term of service in Israel. I told him that I would return home to attend seminary and then come back to the region to work among Arabic-speaking Muslims. He then asked how I came to that decision. I explained that it was nothing that I had decided—the Lord had just put a passion for these people within me, and anything different would mean being disobedient to Him.

He seemed surprised to find a girl who wanted to live in such a strict culture and shared with me the experiences he had seen the girls on his team go through. David then told me of his love for Sudan and some of his adventures. He said that he too felt called back to this area, but didn't know exactly where—just that it was with Arabic-speaking Muslims.

David then began telling me about his enjoyment of hunting and shooting. He said that was one of the reasons he chose to attend West Texas A&M University, so that he could try out for the rifle team. He'd enrolled only to discover the team was disbanded his freshman year. In an effort to join in the conversation, I told him how I loved to watch the Ross Volunteers at Texas A&M practice and perform (West Texas A&M and Texas A&M are separate universities located on opposite sides of the state). The Ross Volunteers were a rifle-carrying performance drill team, not a shooting team (I knew that), but David got all excited about meeting a girl who was interested in watching a rifle shooting team practice. He even e-mailed some of his buddies in the States telling them he'd met a girl who liked to watch the rifle team! Almost a year later, a missionary friend of his popped his bubble by telling him the Ross Volunteers had nothing to do with shooting. But the points I unwittingly made in our Eilat conversation stood me in good stead until David learned the truth. He said by that time it didn't matter—he'd discovered plenty of other positive things to replace his burst girl-who-likes-guns bubble.

As we finished our conversation, we found ourselves at the open-air food court where, in the middle of the eating area, they had cleared tables for a dance floor. They apparently were having a night of folk/line-dancing, Hebrew-style. We watched for a while and then decided to join in on the festivities, though none of us knew any of the steps. I reached into my bag and took out my camera to record the fun. Before I knew it David was out on the floor kicking up his heels—literally.

Now David was one who would never be accused of having lots of grace and poise. Instead, most people lovingly thought of him as a "bull in a china shop." So picture him out on a makeshift dance floor joining the Israelis in a dance that required spinning, jumping, and kicking your legs out, all the while dancing in a circle that is moving to the right.

Soon, this kind lady was trying to give him tips. He just kept going, not caring, and trying to keep up but not take out the people next to him. We were laughing on the sidelines at his willingness to humiliate himself. The song ended and another quickly began. The rest of us ran out to join David. We were laughing and I thought I was doing pretty well, but the man next to me didn't think so and asked me to leave the dance floor. I laughed all the way off—as did my friends, saying I got kicked off the floor! David always liked to bring that up to prove he was a better dancer by asking "Yeah, but I've never been kicked off a dance floor. Have you?" Oh, the humiliation . . . .

One night we stayed up talking with some other people who were also staying at the hostel. There happened to be a man from Sudan who was staying there. David began a conversation with him, and it turned out David had been through the man's village. So there was an immediate connection, aided by the fact that David was conversing in the man's heart language: Sudanese Arabic. David then began telling him a story.

On one trip, David, along with a handful of student volunteers, was out in a remote village and it came time for dinner. This particular village didn't have a restaurant so David had to come up with some way for them to eat. He saw some chickens running out in front of a hut, so he knocked on the door. Can you imagine the surprise of the Sudanese national who opened the door to find an Arabic-speaking Caucasian? David asked if he could buy a chicken. The man was reluctant at first but then consented, asking an outlandish price for a scrawny bird.

David paid for the chicken and went to where they had started a fire to roast their dinner. Not having anticipated that they would be cooking outdoors, they had not brought any cooking gear. So they improvised—with swords. Several of the team members had purchased native swords—not decorative, ceremonial models with dull blades. They had bought the genuine items with sharp blades. David held the chicken down on a rock and stretched out its neck, while one of the others separated the bird from its head with the sword. They cleaned and quartered their victim, skewered the pieces on the sword, and roasted them over the fire.

To the Sudanese man to whom David was telling this story, it seemed normal—just another example of what one does living in a remote village in Sudan. But I was overwhelmed—in a good way! There didn't seem to be anything this man couldn't figure or finagle a way to do. (David told me later his intent in telling the tale was to impress *me*. I laughed, "Well, it worked.")

We enjoyed each other's company the whole weekend while trying not to make it too obvious to one another. As we said our goodbyes, I couldn't help but wonder if our paths would cross again. David headed back to the border crossing to Jordan, and I loaded the van to return to Jerusalem (the borders of Israel and Jordan meet at Eilat). As we drove to the highway we passed him walking to the border crossing and my heart leapt. Something inside me softly whispered, "You'll see him again, don't worry."

A day or two later, I checked my e-mail, and there in my in-box was a note from David. He had written a thank-you note to me and to our group, but included a question in hopes that I would write back. His strategy worked and I replied. From that point, our e-mail correspondence was steady.

David started to keep me posted about his world adventures via e-mail, and our friendship took a *You've Got Mail* direction with a Middle Eastern backdrop. There was an anticipation and excitement in my stomach every time I noticed an e-mail from David. Since his travels would make him often unreachable, the e-mails were like wrapped gifts that I looked forward to savoring in my small cubby.

We quickly worked our way through the elementary matters like, "How did you become a Christian?" "How did you get to Journeyman?" and "How were you called to missions?" Our dialogue moved from reports on our daily activities and highlights of our week to the struggles and difficulties we were dealing with in ministry and life.

We became to each other that person you call when you need someone to pray—someone you not only know will pray but that you know is genuinely concerned, someone who *wants* to pray for you, even about the little things. I was there for him during one of his most trying times of his two years, and he was there for me during the most trying days of my Journeyman tour. I soon found myself making mental notes throughout the day to tell David of things that had happened, a habit that I continued even after we were married.

During this time his e-mails became a highlight of my day. They were encouraging, uplifting, and hilarious! I soon began to struggle with whether we were getting too close—getting too involved with each other personally. Granted, we were living in two different countries and even on different continents at times. Still, I didn't want to let my heart go somewhere it shouldn't—somewhere I hadn't received God's blessing to let it go. And dating was forbidden while on our mission field. It wasn't that we were doing anything remotely near dating, but that was probably because we were separated geographically. My heart was moving to a place that, had we been near one another, would have made me want to spend time with him. I couldn't deny what my heart was telling me.

As I prayed, the Lord put me at ease, assuring me of His guidance and reminding me not to push, to wait and let David take the initiative. David later told me that, at about the same time, he felt the Lord had given him permission to continue initiating a relationship with me. But it was not just permission—more like direction. These changes occurred over several months, but we could both tell our friendship was becoming a true blessing to both of us.

* * *

In October of 2000, things started to heat up in the West Bank, that part of Israel north of Jerusalem and west of the Jordan River. The Palestinians initiated *al-Aqsa intifada*, a horrible season of violence that began when the Palestinian prime minister, Yasser Arafat, walked out of U.S.-led peace talks at Camp David in July. The *intifada* broke loose in September, 2000, when the chairman of Israel's opposition *Likud* party, Ariel Sharon, approached the *al-Aqsa* mosque, or the Dome of the Rock, located on top of the Temple Mount in Jerusalem. The mosque is the third holiest site in the Muslim world.

Imad Falouji, the Palestinian Authority Communications Minister, later said that the violence had been planned in July, far in advance of Sharon's "provocation." Sharon was told by Israel's Internal Security Minister that as long as he didn't enter the mosque, there wouldn't be trouble. Regardless of which came first, and what the motives may or may not have been, the result was disastrous.

Offended Palestinians and Israeli-Arabs took to the streets with rock throwing and chants of *Allah hu akbar* ("Allah is greater!"). Israeli soldiers responded with rubber bullets but switched to live ammunition in an attempt to turn back the mobs. Before long, Palestinians were dying, which only inflamed the conflict. Through 2004, a cycle of Palestinian attacks in Israel and retaliations by the Israeli army left more than 4,000 dead, mostly Palestinians.

I was nearly six hours from the West Bank and most of the trouble, but that did little to console my parents in Texas. They were anxious as the news made it appear as if the whole country of Israel was going up in flames. We, as foreigners, were being briefed on the fine art of avoiding rioters, and I didn't tell my parents about a friend being unable to return home to Nazareth because of the danger. But I had David to confide in, and his e-mails kept me sane. He understood my situation and our lighthearted e-mail banter about Lebanese game shows and riot police in his country of Jordan kept me from focusing on the war zone within Israel.

"Things here, comparatively, are downright boring," David wrote in an e-mail in October of 2000. "However, there is still plenty of tension in the refugee camps here in Jordan and among the population in general (which is about 75% Palestinian). Plus, the big picture is looking unstable, and since the U.S. government is usually over-cautious, that poses problems for us. Today the embassy held a meeting to determine whether or not they're going to evacuate U.S. citizens. It's an optional flight, but our supervisor has already told us that if the embassy evacuates, we will too. We're waiting to hear what their decision was. So we're kind of in limbo right now. But we have our evacuation lists ready and clothes ready to throw in a suitcase if it comes to that. Just another day in the exciting Middle East."

I'd like to say I was witnessing history, but in reality, history was more of a nuisance than anything. Routine walks into town became an ever-changing maze of what sections to avoid that day—the Israelis or the Palestinians. Cars were being burned in the streets, and I had to call friends to see if it was okay to move about safely on any given day. CNN had even started a feature called "Crisis in the Middle East," which detailed the day's events and certainly wasn't helping to calm my parents' nerves.

Secretary of State Madeline Albright became a regular fixture in Jerusalem. Eventually, the talks included UN Secretary Kofi Annan and President Bill Clinton himself, who met with both prime ministers, Israel's Barak and the Palestinian Arafat, and the Egyptian president and Jordan's king. This high-powered summit finally ended with a tentative ceasefire agreement between the Palestinians and the Israelis, and a threat by Barak that Arafat had seventy-two hours to cease the violent protests.

Angered by Barak's threat, Arab leaders held an Arab League summit in Cairo, but it did little, other than provoke more harsh words against Israel. At the time, it felt like such a roller coaster; first there's peace, now there's not. Really, the leaders had only a small amount of power over rioters in the street. And we in the mission field waited for word on a possible evacuation.

Life around me remained routine. In the mornings I scrubbed floors and toilets, and later in the afternoon I worked with young Arab women, teaching them English as a second language. My relationships with the young women were now very strong, and we would spend countless hours baking, shopping, and drinking coffee at the local café.

In Jordan, where David was stationed, it remained relatively calm because King Abdullah outlawed protests in the street. Armored personnel carriers became a frequent and welcome sight, especially around the flashpoints of Israeli and American embassies.

King Abdullah's orders were followed, and Jordan had only a small amount of activity relating to the *intifada*, but in Israel things got worse. Israelis fired missiles from helicopter gunships into Palestinian positions, and Palestinians responded by killing two Israeli soldiers in Ramallah and dragging their bodies through the streets of town. We had missionary friends in Ramallah, and we waited to get word of their safety. These friends waited too long to evacuate, and when the Israeli soldiers were killed, the city went into lockdown and they were trapped in their house. Violence waged in the streets in front of their home, while they hid behind closed curtains and locked doors. We waited and prayed. Given the mob violence in Ramallah, it wasn't safe for anyone to move around, especially Americans. Finally, a Palestinian friend helped them out under cover of night, and they escaped unharmed. The U.S. government's overzealous evacuation plans didn't seem quite as ridiculous after that narrow escape, and we listened closely to our government's warnings, waiting for life to return to normal.

During this time, the USS *Cole* was attacked off the coast of Yemen, killing seventeen Americans. It was as if those who wanted war, or *jihad*, hoped to involve the world powers and make their presence and their plight known.

David was struck by how many countries were paralyzed by the inner workings of the Israeli-Palestinian battle: "It's such a far-reaching war. Both sides, the Israelis and the Palestinians, are full of hate. Both sides have killed people, including the innocent."

David and I remained confused on the issue, but confident that God was in control. We just prayed that the violence and the hate would stop soon. With the added security, David and I continued our e-mail friendship, and I kept him aware of the current situation in my town. He found it hard to believe that with only the Jordan River to separate our countries, his remained outside the war while Israel battled onward with the Palestinians.

In a nearby town some Jewish youths attacked Arab shops in a local mall. Our town remained safe, but everyone was tense. Small acts of teenage vandalism took on the utmost importance, because you never knew what might ignite tensions. The waiting was miserable.

I was feeling quiet and a bit melancholy and ready to leave if war broke out, but I continued to go about my daily life, trying my best to keep the children shielded from the situation outside the village. The buses had stopped running into the Arab villages, so life was slower than ever. I learned during this time how important my daily spiritual disciplines were. There was nothing I could personally do to impact the countries fighting each other, but I could be faithful where God had put me. I was finally seeing that my job scrubbing toilets gave glory to His name. By faith, I got on my hands and knees and scrubbed and mopped the same floors. Outside, *intifada* raged, but within my shipping container, I was learning to be quiet amidst the storm.

In contrast, David was embarking on a trip to the Sudan. We both found it odd that the "safety" of Sudan, a country in the middle of its own fifty-year civil war and accusations of genocide, would be considered the better option at the time. But so it was, and so David went.

CHAPTER SIX

Pretty Dadgum Kwayis

Pretty dadgum *kwayis*." David said this all the time. In his combination country-boy-Arabic-speak it meant "pretty darned good." That's exactly how he felt about all things Sudanese.

Every time he set out for a visit to the Sudan, he was like a kid in a candy store: rife with anticipation for the adventure. Nothing made David happier than life in the Sudan and touching the Arab people with Christianity, whether that meant a prayer walk around the town or a discussion on how their religions differed. He was especially intrigued by the places never touched by the gospel, by the areas that most Americans would never visit. Northern Sudan was definitely one of those areas.

Sudan is located directly south of Egypt and above (to the northwest of) Ethiopia, and combines both the Arab and African cultures to form its own unique society. The Nile River runs through Sudan, giving it a distinctly African feel, and Port Sudan is a major trade city, located on the Red Sea where more modern trade takes place and scuba divers come to visit. There are many Asians (mostly Chinese) in this area, as China has a major stake in the oil trade with

Sudan. Being a port city, Port Sudan has a distinctly international flavor. All told, there are over 33 million residents of the Sudan.

Since Sudan's independence in 1956, a civil war has waged between the Sudanese government forces (National Islamic Front regime) and several different black African groups that combine many different religions, including Islam. For the most part, radical Islam has not been embraced by the people groups—just the government. The people's Islam tends to be more laid-back and approached with a sense of moderation. The fundamentalist branch of Islam has had a hard time finding its place among the casual lifestyle of the African people. But the government hopes to put an end to that by force.

In 2004, Sudan's air force bombed several cities, and over a million people were driven from their homes into Darfur, the western region. It was reported that a thousand people a day were dying there. While the UN argued over whether or not the NIF's slaughter amounted to genocide, civilians continued to die.

On a broad scale, what's happening in Sudan is far worse than Israel or Iraq or any other nation engaged in war. Millions are dying, and the discovery of oil in 1978 has only made matters worse. The oil is located in the Christian part of the country, which has led to more bloodshed. The NIF continues its rampage. The ethnic cleansing taking place at the hands of the radical Muslim (government) forces makes it seem akin to Nazi Germany leading up to World War II. Sudan is no vacation spot, and David took great care to keep a low profile when visiting the country.

David arrived in El Obeid in central Sudan in October, 2000, before much of the killing was known to the general public. But it was always present, and David used to say the Sudan had a "dark feel." Oppression hung in the air like a suffocating cloud. David was anxious to get down to business on this particular trip and watch the Arabic-African culture in play again.

The city of El Obeid is large and sprawling—a classic example of Third World African towns. It boasts dirt streets, beat-up cars, and women carrying goods on their heads. David would sit in a road-side café and take in all the sights like one might take in a beautiful beach scene. He felt as though he was "on safari" while he sat in the midst of the sights and took notes on all he'd seen and what needs were most prominent in the villages. He hadn't quite gotten used to Sudanese dining at this point, and he often lamented how he missed the "southern" hospitality in Jordan and the Arab food he'd grown to love. But it wouldn't be long before David actually preferred being in the Sudan and relished the goat livers as if they were a Big Mac.

With David's first visits, he felt the Arab-Africans "circled the wagons" and made it difficult for him to engage them in conversation to assess their needs—much more so than in the Middle East Arab countries. Still, that didn't stop the extroverted David from making his presence known and finding allies within the country. After a few trips, those feelings quickly evaporated, as he became more accustomed to the population.

On this particular trip into El Obeid, David met a group of Russians who worked as pilots in the region. From them he learned what it was like to work as a foreigner in Sudan. Igor* brought out a crystal bottle full of "wodka" and called it "a special drink for us." It was special all right—a rancid yellow color with limes floating on the top. When David declined to partake, his new Russian friends thought him rude. But he chose the benefits of long-term common sense over short-term relationships. "Nyet," David said, while they tried to pour. "Nyet," he repeated. All the while Igor tried to extend his offer. David and his team stayed in the Russians' home for a couple of hours, having the most basic of political discussions. The Russian pilots knew only enough English to land a plane (mostly numbers).

"Israel, problem?" David would ask.

"No problem," the heavily-accented answer came back.

"Turkey, problem?"

"No problem," Igor would answer. Victor would just give a thumbs-up or thumbs-down for the country David inquired about. It was rudimentary, but the kind of language that risk-taking men from different countries understood without a lot of embellishments.

David was a cultivator—the person who went in ahead of the seed-sowers to assess the condition of the "soil." Every time he went in with a team, he went to a new and previously unsurveyed city, recording information that made life easier, more efficient, and more productive for those who followed and established long-term works.

David and his team were concerned with the humanitarian needs in central Sudan and made arrangements to take the team into the deepest parts of the country. The only transportation into these areas is a lorry (think of a big, American dump truck packed with supplies). Lorries do not run on a schedule that works if you're in a hurry. If it's supposed to leave at 2:00 p.m., it will probably leave closer to 5:00 p.m. In this part of Africa, time is relative.

David was a patient man who enjoyed the ever-changing variables of travel in foreign countries—including waiting. Delays were an opportunity to strike up a conversation, an endeavor at which he excelled. As they prepared to leave El Obeid to move further into the country, David grew concerned with the lateness of the hour. The later they left, the greater the chance they'd be traveling in the cold night air in the open-air lorry.

A ride on a lorry is anything but comfortable. You are perched high atop whatever cargo the lorry is carrying—in this case, logs—bouncing up and down over incredibly bumpy roads. If you have seen pictures of travelers riding on freight trains in India—hanging on the sides, perched atop the cars—you've got the idea of travel-by-lorry. This lorry was packed with people sitting high above the ground on the logs. In the cab were the driver and a guard riding shotgun—though in this case, the guard was riding AK-47. Seeing this was not a confidence-builder for David, though given Sudan's tumultuous and violent history, he was glad to be traveling with an armed guard.

Ever the optimist, David focused on the beautiful scenery as the lorry chugged along over the dirt roads. Plenty of trees, grass, and bushes dotted the landscape with many butte-like hills—a big difference from the desert he was used to. As he rolled past grass-hut villages, he reveled in the wilds of Africa's backcountry, seeing things that were completely new. He wrote long entries in his journal to pass the time, making notes of all he saw, and even drawing little huts or African women's hairstyles to remember them or better explain them at future speaking engagements.

When the lorry stopped for dinner at a grass-hut restaurant, David struck up a conversation with a man named Mohammed from the *Dongolawi* tribe. As they sipped African tea, they discussed religion and Mohammed's tribe. These were the small moments that made the long, difficult trips easier for David. He loved meeting people and hearing about how they lived their lives.

After a filling supper of chicken and *foul* (pronounced "fool"—similar to our refried beans but with the addition of raw egg, a bit of garlic, salt, and lemon), a dish David found "dadgum *laziiz*" (delicious), they got back on the lorry, this time with several new passengers. Now the five members of their team were squeezed, making room for the additional riders. David hunkered down for the long, cold night ahead.

As the sun sank beneath the western horizon, the sky turned cold and the wind bitter. The five team members, three men and two women, curled up into a ball to conserve body heat. But as the ride went on, the lorry kept stopping, and each time, more people would climb onto the truck. Underneath them, the load of logs started shifting and then gave way with a loud *crack!*

As the logs broke apart, David tumbled four feet down onto the diesel cans stacked under the logs. His new position under the logs was warmer and he thought about staying put, but decided he'd be safer, albeit a lot colder, up with the rest of the team. They pulled him back to the top of the pile—and all while the lorry continued rumbling along, the driver unaware of what had happened. The rest of the cold and miserable riders looked at David with disdain at his obvious lack of lorry experience. About the only way for an American to be prepared for this kind of travel would be to leave a rodeo gate in Fort Worth on a bucking bronco and ride it as far as Houston.

The team wrapped themselves in their sleeping bags to withstand the cold night air, praying their stop would be the next one announced.

The team rolled into the first town at 3:00 a.m. and found lots of people milling about in anticipation of the lorry's arrival. The logs shifted again, and this time Amy* tumbled over backwards into a crowd of people eight feet below. There was much commotion among the natives at the inexperienced American woman who didn't know how to stay on top of the lorry, but she emerged from the crowd unharmed.

Arriving without incident in the next small town, the team checked into a grass-hut hotel which David found better than the

Ritz after the long, cramped ride on the logs. There were plenty of restaurants in the town, and only the bombers flying overhead and the ever-present AK-47s reminded them that they weren't on a mini-vacation now that they were off the truck.

The respite was short-lived, as a new lorry awaited them the following morning to take them to a smaller village, further into the center of Africa. Climbing onto the new lorry with less excitement this time, the team rode for hours until they stopped at a little tea shack along the dirt road, where they ordered tea and *foul*. The two women on the team struck up a conversation with two *Kabbabiish* women (the *Kabbabiish* are a tribe in Sudan) in the tea house, while the men were surrounded by men in long *jalabiyas*, traditional Muslim robes.

Two of the men were the *sheiks* (leaders) of the village and they wanted to know why the team had come. David explained briefly that they were there to assess needs for the area. To take the focus off the team, David then asked the *sheiks* about the famed *Darb el-arbein*, the Forty-Days Road. This was the longest and most treacherous of trade routes that had once been the primary trade artery from Sudan into Egypt. It was a few days away by lorry and was an obvious source of pride for the people.

The *sheik* explained that the camel market is a huge business in Sudan; it's second only to Chad in camel production. For centuries, camel caravans used the Forty-Days Road to transport goods to Cairo where the goods were sold, along with many of the camels. The caravans then returned to Sudan loaded down with paper, whalebone, balsam oil, and other specialty commodities. Sudan still exports camels along this route that conjures up romantic images of centuries past. The *sheik* was delighted to share about his country's pride and David listened with rapt attention. The team was set to visit a camel market, and now David looked forward to knowing more about the business. David's interest and the *sheiks'* pride soon bound the men together in friendship, and they carried on comfortably.

The longer the team talked and asked questions of the local men, the larger the crowd became. Word spread fast that Arabic-speaking *khawajas* (foreigners) were in town, but it soon became apparent that the Arab men weren't threatened by the men in David's team. David realized riding the lorry had been worth it, because no one had ever visited the area before. Their visit provided a foot in the door to this particular region. Sudan was known for its violent geopolitical realities, but David only saw opportunity. The people were so friendly and open to relief help that he was dumbfounded that there weren't more workers in the field there. He hoped his team's trip would provide information to excite future relief workers and open the door for the gospel to be spread.

Their final destination on this trip was to a major village that had yet to be assessed for needs. It turned out to be a large city, which wasn't expected. Restaurants lined the streets. The town boasted a hospital, pharmacy, bank, three schools, and even a veterinarian. The people lived in grass huts with a tin shack for the collective toilets. It was good for the team to see how well the city did without intervention, but there were still great needs. The following day consisted of meetings with the area leaders. The meetings went so well that David kept waiting for the other shoe to drop. Certainly, the quest should be more difficult than a hard lorry ride. But the people were quite willing to have help and hoped David and his team might be a source.

The team inspected the town's wells and noted that water was the greatest need. The town had two "donkey wells"—forty feet deep with mechanical pumps to bring the water up. The water was clean—there just wasn't enough of it. There were only two of these wells to service the entire town. This was clearly not enough to sustain current needs, much less accommodate future growth.

After a few days, the team grew convinced that this area was wide open for relief workers. Relief aid would be more than welcomed—it would be gratefully received. In 1985 there had been a deadly flood and the American government sent in bread and grain. The people remembered and called the bread "Reagan" in honor of the former president who made it possible. So the door had already been opened for receiving Americans.

On the way back to town after the day of meetings and away from his peer group, Mohammed, their guide for the day, began asking questions about God. Specifically, he wanted to know if Jesus could forgive any sin. He wasn't interested for himself—he just wanted to know about the religion that had been forbidden in his area. The conversation gave the team hope. They knew the area needed Living Water, as well as the liquid kind.

After meetings and copious note-taking, the team boarded a lorry for its final destination: extreme western Sudan, or Darfur. This was the region now associated with alleged ethnic cleansing, government bombings, torture, rape, and other atrocities at the hands of the National Islamic Front. David trembled at the idea, both from anticipation and fear of the unknown.

CHAPTER SEVEN

Intifada in Israel—Into the Deep Sudan

While David was visiting a danger zone in Sudan, I was immersed in one of my own, back in the Arab-Israeli section of Israel. Miles away, the West Bank continued to be full of fireworks, though things had calmed down slightly. People were beginning to venture out like they did before the strife began, including me—I felt comfortable moving about and traveling some distance from my village. But CNN's daily "Crisis in the Middle East" reports on Israel's violence had already caused much of the country to empty of foreigners.

Living as a missionary in an area where the gospel cannot be freely preached is sometimes hard. Visiting teams of Christian workers were my main source of fellowship. This is how I came to know Beth Moore, a Bible teacher and author who came to Israel to tape a new study series. Along with some of my Journeymen friends, I spent two weeks traveling to various locations in Israel with Beth and her team. Before that trip, I had known Beth only as a conference speaker, and I had a great respect for her teaching. From the outset, Beth's entire team nurtured and cared for our group of young women who were so far from home and so hungry for fellowship. Beth personally poured herself into our lives during those two weeks, ministering to our hearts that were so much in need of the refreshment she freely gave. Her friendship came to epitomize sacrificial love to me when we met again later in the States.

One of the sad realities about the national believers is that they weren't welcoming of international Christian workers. I once had a Christian friend tell me she was going to attend a women's retreat, only to quickly say she couldn't invite me. They didn't want foreigners on the trip. I convinced myself it was to avoid the language and translation issues, but I came to believe there were deeper cross-cultural issues at work as well.

E-mail was our other form of communication with other Christians. With David in Sudan, his e-mails became more erratic, and without the fellowship of the visiting teams, I was starting to feel left out in the wilderness. Life went on as normal for non-natives like me—we avoided certain parts of town and learned to be more aware of our surroundings. I wasn't sad or anxiously awaiting David's return. I was just tired of the media reports portraying the Middle East as a place most of us didn't recognize.

My ministry, teaching Arabic women English, continued to bear fruit, as did my work with the children in the foster home and my social life with my Arab "adopted families." But I still missed David's uplifting e-mails, and seeing his address in my in-box.

When I e-mailed David about my disappointment at a visiting team being cancelled, he wrote back, "We had a volunteer group scheduled to come to Eritrea (a small northeast country on the coast of Africa along the Red Sea), but just three months before they were to come, full-scale war broke out as Ethiopia invaded western Eritrea. We're talking bombing runs, tanks, land mines, and a whole mess of other things generally detrimental to a volunteer group's safety. However, being an obscure Third World country, no one in the States knew anything about the war. Oh sure, we warned them about it but told them not to worry, and sure enough, three weeks before they flew in, a ceasefire was signed and Ethiopia withdrew. Four weeks later, I was standing with six volunteers in the remains of a bombed-out hotel that Ethiopian fighters had destroyed in their siege on the city. When it comes to war, the bottom line is, 'no publicity, no problem.'"

I wrote to David continuously while he was in the Sudan that October. He'd answer me as he got Internet access in a small café somewhere along his route. I stayed busy cleaning the foster home and writing a newsletter to let my prayer team back in America know how things were going. I was teaching English to Druze Arabs and wanted prayer support for the ministry. One day during all this, I decided it was time to escape the confines of my container's walls. Cabin fever had also struck my roommate Susie* and we planned a much-needed trip into the Jewish section of Israel, the most westernized portion of the country.

We planned a Saturday visit into town to get some money to pay a bill and got stuck in *Shabbat* (Sabbath) traffic. I thought about David baking in the sun, riding atop lorries filled with onions, and decided that having access to Subway sandwiches and window displays of Depend undergarments was just what I needed to lift my spirits.

Getting out of my part of town brought more freedoms: a girl could talk to a boy without long-term consequences; we could wear shorts if we wanted or play baseball and not be thought the worse for it. We could hit baseballs on a pitching machine or practice the guitar in public. It just meant letting your guard down for a time. I never lamented anything I gave up to be in Israel, because I loved my work and the relationships I made there. But going into the more westernized parts of Israel was like being released for a time to get back to my normal, outgoing self. I am innately an off-the-chart extrovert, but that personality does not work for females in the male-dominated Arab society. So I learned to tone it down significantly. However, even with the new, toned-down me, it felt great to have a time of freedom in Israel.

As the Israeli-Palestinian conflict cooled down, missionaries who had left the country came flooding back. The practical necessities of an agrarian culture overtook the violence. Snipers hiding in the olive trees had to come down as the olive-picking season began and harvesting the crops became the priority. Arabs in my area of Israel were busy picking olives and had no time for conflict. Since where I lived had not suffered much from the violence anyway, it wasn't much of a change. But all over Israel the temperature was cooling off.

At home in the States, the election fiasco of 2000, where the country had yet to pick a winner, took its toll on Americans living in other countries. The world predicted doom and gloom for America because the country could not unite on a president; a loss of power was spoken of with glee on television. I knew our government had its checks and balances, and I wasn't worried about the long-term outcome or its implications for the United States. But it did get old listening to the prophecies by countless news organizations in Israel, just as it did hearing about the Israeli crisis on CNN. I guess dirty laundry flaps in breezes that blow from both directions.

At the same time, one of my fellow workers left the orphanage and went back to her home in Holland. Anne's* absence affected me deeply because she'd been like a sister to me during our time in the container. Though I missed Anne, I still enjoyed having David to vent to via e-mail. Knowing my true feelings and ultimate desire to serve, I felt completely safe sharing my thoughts with him: "It's a hard-knock life for us," I wrote, quoting from the *Annie* soundtrack, about my daily cleaning, just like the little orphan Annie. David, of course, was living his own hard-knock life, riding on lorries full of steaming onions in the heat of the day. I had no idea then that he was on his way into Darfur, spiritually one of the darkest places in Sudan.

David was visiting an authentic camel market in the Sudan. He was bartering in Arabic for beads, glad-handing the merchants, and making enjoyable videotapes that we watched later. He narrated his tour as though he was a CNN correspondent, and every time he mentioned Sudan he would say, "the largest country in Africa." He thought it was hilarious that so many people don't realize Africa isn't a country, but a continent. So he took every opportunity to be the teacher.

Contrary to the lighthearted banter in the videotapes, life in the Sudan was closing in on David. He was starting to feel down-trodden, even depressed. The tone of his e-mails started to worry me, because I knew if the ever-optimistic David could be discouraged, it was not going well.

The cultural stress of rough, primitive traveling for two weeks took its toll on the entire team. They arrived in Al Fashir, a city in western Sudan, and the eventual site of much unrest and alleged genocide by government forces. After another rough night of harsh conditions on the lorry, the first hotel in Al Fashir proved to be too primitive for the now-exhausted team. Knowing David, I thought if the hotel was too primitive for him, it was basically uninhabitable.

The team looked for a new hotel the second night. They found a government rest house with real toilets and green grass in front of the rooms. It was a time of reflection for David, as his body was spiritually and physically spent. The team had truly reached their limits with days on a cramped lorry and water assessment trips that kept them on their feet until dark. They settled in the hotel, and decided a day of rest was necessary. *Even the Lord took an occasional day off,* they reasoned.

"After all day resting and taking it easy in relatively comfortable surroundings, I was starting to come out of my fetal position," David said. "It's hard at times like this to fathom why I'm here. I mean, why am I putting up with this? Why am I riding on lorries? Why am I spending the night freezing, wrapped up in a tube (sleeping bag)? Why am I staying in 'hole' hotels and eating *foul?* It's tough and it's hard. It's also hard not to see any fruit in my work, so at times like this, doubts begin to fill your head."

These words of David's really showed me the depth of his despair but also his willingness to serve. If there was anything that defined David, it was good food and social surroundings. He'd sacrificed not only the life he relished in the States, but also the great food and Arab hospitality of Jordan. His spirit was really damaged by the time he got to Al Fashir, Sudan.

Al Fashir, in the Darfur region, was the site of all-out war in February of 2003. Nearly three years to the day from when David had been there with his team, water purification engineers were gunned down, murdered by government forces. Although David's visit took place before these horrible incidents, all the ingredients were in place. The area is spiritually dark and, right now, nearly uninhabitable, as many of its residents fled to Chad or other regions of the Sudan after fighting broke out. David felt this darkness and his emotions were getting the better of him. I prayed my heart out for him at the time, and I just wanted God's will to be done. But I'll also admit I wanted him back in the relative safety of Jordan. More importantly, I wanted his zeal for life to return.

Hearing the broken spirit within him brought me down. David was forever upbeat, and this turn scared me as he thought about what to do. Though I hadn't experienced the fatigue of seemingly endless lorry rides and sleeping in huts or the dangers of the Sudan, I understood his struggle. I was very familiar with spiritual darkness and the desire to see tangible fruit from your labor. Anyone who has worked on the mission field understands those days where you question the work, question the outcome, and wonder if it is all worth it. I wanted to help David through this, because I had been there myself.

At this point in his trip, David actually questioned whether he should stay in the Sudan or head back home to the relative normalcy of Jordan. He worked out the positives and negatives on a sheet and really tried to pray through the crisis of faith he was having. He wrote:

Why Stay?

Spend more time in Sudan; get better acquainted with the area and its people.

Go north with Mark and further investigate the country.

Why?

Help with his work.

Want to help.

Don't want to be seen as a quitter.

It makes me a team player.

See more of Sudan.

Why not?

Potential security problems.

Don't have peace about the stay.

Spend more time with Sudanese friends.

Finalize Camel Treks.

Why Leave?
Rest.
Avoid burn-out.
See Lee before he returns to the States.
See friends in Jordan.

David decided to return to Jordan. His spirit was dry and he needed restoration before he returned to eastern Sudan. He and his team found their way back into Khartoum to plan for a visiting team coming the following summer, and then he returned to his home base.

My own spirit was in deep need of refreshing. I'd been meeting with my fourth supervisor since I'd started as a Journeyman in Israel. The meetings went well, but even the meeting place was a source of fear, as the supervisor was male and single. Although he was nearly twice my age, my friends in the Arab section of town would not understand such a meeting. I prayed for protection from being seen, which God granted. As we discussed my current situation—my lack of ministry with the children and serving more as a maid—I realized I was also in a place of discovery for my ministry future. I'd come up with my own thriving ministry with the Israeli-Arab women, but it needed to be addressed formally by the staff paying my salary. I'd created solid and deep relationships with the women around me, so perhaps it was time to pour more of myself into that rather than cleaning. Oddly enough, it was Thanksgiving time that David and I were both going through our laments.

A new German team member at the orphanage continued to be strident in his views. He was almost Pharisaical in his views of Christianity: "I cannot live among heathens like you who don't cover their heads when they pray and watch television and use the Internet." I felt like the *Twilight Zone* music played whenever he came into view. He asked why I "defiantly" refused to cover my head during prayer. It was always something. Using Scripture, I explained to him why I didn't cover my head, but he suggested I use a straw hat. So, to keep the peace, I wrote to David, "While you're out at the camel market, if you see a straw hat suitable for prayer, be sure and pick it up for me—I'll reimburse you."

Israeli military jets were beginning to fly over the Palestinian zones, and I held my breath as I thought about what might be coming. We waited for word on the street as to what was going on with the conflict. In the meantime, Anne and I took a trip to Caesarea as a celebration of her time at the orphanage and her impending departure. We did little more than tour the ruins and take in a movie, but the break was fruitful. I returned refreshed and ready to work side by side with my German "friend."

I had only six months left in my assignment in Israel, and I was having trouble communicating with the owners of the foster home. I saw so many possibilities, so much more that could be done in the ministry, and I wanted more for the children. The owners wanted me to do my cleaning, and let them handle the management of the orphanage. In truth, we wanted the same things—we just had different ideas about how to go about it. I felt a desire to change things for the next visiting missionaries who came to overtake my cleaning duties. Although we all had good intentions for the ministry, many of them were falling under the weight of "busyness" on everyone's part. I hoped to solve those problems with written plans before I left the country and returned home to Texas for a Christmas respite.

David, meanwhile, was traveling the harsh desert road from Port Sudan to Khartoum, planning his future while riding atop the onions. He was thankful for the dependability of the lorry, however, as after a few tire blowouts on the way from Khartoum, their rented Land Cruiser would shake and shimmy at high speeds. David took the time to write a song about the experience to the music of "Cruising Along in My Automobile:"

Limping along in my automobile,
got me a couple of warbling wheels . . .
Get up to 80 (km), it starts to dance,
I think I'm gonna wet my pants . . .
Hail, hail Land Cruiser, you make me feel like such a loser.

Obviously, it was a long ride. And this trip on the lorry turned out to be a trip of luxury compared to previous ones. The five members of David's team were the only passengers, as the desert treks across the parched lands were not very popular. They sat under the merciless desert sun, atop a load of baking onions, lumbering along at about fifteen miles per hour. They crossed right through the heart of *Beja* country, which was little more than a wasteland. Even camels shunned the land, and the few they saw sought shade wherever it could be found.

The *Beja* are a nomadic people group, with a million and a half members who mostly live in the northeastern portion of Sudan. Most of them are herders of sheep and goats. Their lifestyle was fascinating to David because they still live in tents. They love music and have kept their own culture despite brief interactions with Christianity and Islam. Although Islam is prevalent in their society, the *Beja* are primarily nomads and their own culture comes first. Those *Beja* who have settled down in one place and don't live the nomadic lifestyle are more likely to embrace Islam, though usually the five pillars of the religion are not practiced—especially the pilgrimage to Mecca. Because this group is so infrequently visited, David's trek through their land caused some fear and trepidation. He stayed prayed up and current in his Bible reading as they tiptoed through the *Beja* territory.

He took comfort in the fact that the lorry and the driver were well-prepared and equipped for wilderness travel. When the lorry would get bogged down in the deep sand, the driver would simply reach for two long tin metal sheets, or "lorry tracks," stick them under the rear wheels for traction and away they'd go. Then, when they'd stop to rest under a patch of shade at a roadside shack, they were provided with tomatoes, cucumbers, bread, and even meat for supper.

When the cover of darkness came, and David's team was full from the meal, he started to relax more and think about his future and whether it included the Sudan. With all of the places David traveled, he remembered Port Sudan as one of the hottest places he'd ever visited. The day he arrived, it was 107 degrees with the humidity off the Red Sea making it nearly unbearable. It wasn't exactly the place to plan his future. But the Sudan trip was coming to an end and he had less than one hundred days left of his Journeyman experience. It was time to make some decisions.

After a bus ride back to Kassala and a trip to the *souq* (market) to buy *Beja* souvenirs, David met his first Christian believer in the marketplace. He even spoke English! The man was from Eritrea, dressed in a *jalabiya,* or traditional Muslim robe, and spoke openly of his love for Jesus. David and his team were a bit nervous to hear the Name so openly spoken and became fearful the man might be a *mukhabarat,* or informer, so they said little of their own faith and said their goodbyes as soon as possible.

David was fascinated by the *Beja* and loved learning more about their culture. But he had to start thinking about his immediate plans—specifically, what to do about seminary back in the States. He was torn over whether to leave then and start seminary in the spring of 2001, or return to the Sudan and the *Beja* people, saving money for seminary in the fall.

CHAPTER EIGHT

Back to Civilization

Late 2000

David returned to the "plush" life in Jordan, and his first visit was to Burger King for some "good ol' American food." He did not miss the fried goat meat and cold beans that were staples in Sudan and greatly appreciated the homemade spaghetti dinner prepared for him by a career missionary family upon his return.

Through his e-mails, I sensed David's spirits lift upon his return to Jordan—just in time for a real Thanksgiving meal of turkey, dressing, mashed potatoes, and even cranberries. This is where the decision for a quick return to the Sudan was slowed a bit.

Leaving Sudan relieved a lot of stress for him, and his roommates surrounded him when he got back into the country. They'd taken to calling him *"Ya Saa'id Mushkalji"* (Mr. Troublemaker). This was because after his first long trip to Sudan he had taken a trip into nearby Turkey for some R&R, only to sleep through a major earthquake on his first day (after which he'd spent the rest of his vacation time assisting aid workers dispensing emergency supplies to the earthquake victims). Another time, he and his team were shot at in Eritrea. There was also a run-in with police in Egypt, and then, of course, his last hard visit with the long lorry rides into the darkest parts of the Sudan.

"I should now be able to qualify for some kind of organizational medal—something like 'Mr. Unlucky' or 'Blackballed in the Most Countries,'" David confessed. His supervisor even suggested he develop a flow chart comparing the hospitality, effectiveness, and general efficiency of the authorities in the many countries where he'd encountered trouble.

"Right now, I'd have to say the guys in Sudan would be leading the hospitality list. However, it was in Sudan that I got shoved into a concrete wall by a power-trip boy with a pistol in his left hand. That would definitely count against them in the hospitality column."

This is an example from one of David's e-mails of how he earned his "Mr. Troublemaker" label: "A coworker and I traveled in the wilderness of North Africa. Sure, we had a map, but it wasn't the most reliable. We got onto this road and headed in the right direction. Suddenly, we saw some men with guns up ahead. It wasn't a rare sight, but it was still unnerving. They yelled at us to stop, but for all we knew they were bandits—so we kept driving. Then they yelled again and sprayed a round of gunfire over the hood of our truck. So, we stopped. Gunfire will do that.

"They came up to the car, mind you, and we still didn't know if they were bandits or not, and even if they weren't, it didn't mean they were good guys. So they approached us, guns aimed at us, asking why we didn't stop. Then they wanted to see our papers and the letters for allowing us on this road. Apparently, we had gotten onto a military road we weren't supposed to be on, and in Northern Sudan this is not a safe place to be. Of course, we didn't know that. Map didn't say it, and the compass had pointed us in the right direction.

"We showed them the papers we had which, of course, didn't satisfy them. So they pointed their guns at us and demanded we get out of the truck. And like my momma always taught me: do what the men with guns ask.

"They made me get back in the truck but told my friend to stay with them. One of them got in the back seat of the truck and, with gun pointed at me, told me to proceed down the road—which, of course, I did. Not knowing where this scenario was leading, I began to pray in English out loud. This angered my captor since he didn't know what I was saying, so I switched to speaking to him in Arabic and continued to pray silently. Once we arrived at the outpost where the soldier's superiors could check my papers, I explained again our situation. They seemed to buy my story—two lost relief workers whose maps led them into an off-limits military area—and I was taken back to where I had left my friend.

"When I arrived, I discovered he had been treated to tea and refreshments (the Arab hospitality never quits) and had taken a nap! So I was riding around in the desert with a gun in my back and he was enjoying tea and cookies with the locals."

Reflecting on his Sudan trip, David was not seeing how taking a bucket bath and eating goat intestines was advancing the kingdom of God—sort of the same phase I'd been through with scrubbing toilets. In his nearly two years David hadn't seen any legitimate fruit from his labor—people coming to Christ—but he noted that he was officially on the rebound: "My faith is rooted in the fact that God is the Lord of the Harvest and He will bring the fruit in His time. I don't understand it all and at times I really question if I'm doing the right thing. But He is Sovereign and nothing happens apart from His control. Praise the Lord!"

Now that so much time has passed, I can see how David was a cultivator, turning up the soil and getting it ready for others to come behind and sow the seeds of the gospel.

While David and I both worked on long-term decision-making, back home in America our country had yet to decide on a president. The race had been deemed "too close to call" between Al Gore and George W. Bush. David was pushing for George W. because he'd interviewed the Republican candidate during his tenure as a reporter in Texas, when Bush was governor of the state, and thought he would like to be able to casually say, "Yeah, I interviewed him once." He'd also interviewed both Barbara Bush and Laura Bush.

I'd even seen George W. Bush when he came to Texas A&M University for the opening of his father's presidential library. And, of course, I was a Texan! But we waited, along with the rest of the world, to see who the new president would be.

Israel continued its quest to keep a lid on the unrest in its country, and we stayed holed up in the foster home as much as possible. The Hebrew University banned political activity of any sort, which resulted in bitter, but silent, protests from those who saw the ban as violating the right to free speech. Rather than waiting forever for things to be resolved in Israel, I planned a trip home to the United States for Christmas. David got his break in Jordan, but I needed the familiarity of Texas. We continued to e-mail each other as often as possible now that he was home in Jordan, and my heart leapt when I'd see his e-mail address on my computer screen. I'd finally been able to admit that his presence was something I missed. I wrote in my journal at the time:

"Thus far, David has intrigued me, made me laugh, encouraged me, and caused me to question what will happen with us later down the road. But tonight, he touched a portion of my heart, and that scares me. It scares me because I never really thought a boy could do that. But through my being scared, it is precious to me because he did not touch my heart by silly compliments or such, but it was through the encouragement that he gave in You, Lord, through a prayer in e-mail. Oh Lord, am I falling too quickly? Is it okay to feel this way about him?"

I focused on the trip to Texas. The very idea made me smile until my face hurt. I couldn't wait to get back home, to see my family and embrace my young nephew, and get away from the daily tension that's simply a part of mission life.

Before I left, the Arab community was deeply involved in the traditions of Ramadan holidays. It was a hard time to be a Christian in the Arab world. At no time is the clash between cultures more apparent than during the Ramadan fast. The Ramadan fast is a commemoration of the first verses of the Koran being given by Allah to Muhammad. It is a celebration of their spiritual reformation.

Strict adherence to the fast includes no eating, drinking, smoking, or sexual relations during the daylight hours. At nightfall, they may resume normal activities. The object is to practice self-control and have a time of spiritual reflection, prayer, and obedience to Allah. At the end of the time, alms are generally given to those poorer than they.

Although the point of the holy days is spiritual renewal, it's also a time in history when Allah supposedly granted battle victories, and so it can often be a time of violence. Because of the war history, often terrorists are incited to start *jihad* during Ramadan, and the violence levels rise. I hoped to leave Israel before any such Ramadan-induced violence occurred.

On December 10, 2000, I received an e-mail from my supervisor basically stating "What you need to do in case we have a war." Tickets out of Israel became like tickets to the Super Bowl: everybody wanted them and nobody could get them. I can't say I was truly worried. No one around me seemed concerned, and the newspapers ran the warnings so often they fell on deaf ears. I was more nervous for David in Cairo traffic. We laughed that it was the live version of the video game "Frogger."

But there was a more serious side to the impending war and the fear that accompanied Ramadan. We never took that for granted, as lighthearted as we tried to be to mask our fears. We weren't only planning for "just in case" situations, but preparing for them. Israel's citizens were getting fitted for gas masks, learning to take special routes to the airport or ports. Of course, we learned to go on with life, making adjustments where necessary. That's what the rest of the country had to do—those who didn't have the option of hopping on a plane to head for a safer place. There were times when being a foreigner was a distinct advantage.

CHAPTER NINE

Christmas 2000—New Year 2001

Israel, Texas, Jordan, Ethiopia

While I worked on getting home to Texas for Christmas, David contemplated career missionary work and how that would affect when he'd go to seminary. He would begin 2001 by visiting Cairo twice, then Ethiopia, and then go back to America. First, however, he'd go skiing in Lebanon for Christmas—not because he was an avid skier, but because he liked the sound of it: "Yeah, my buddies and I went skiing in Lebanon . . . ." Pure David—He was always willing to try something new.

David's hard work as a Journeyman had not gone unnoticed by his superiors. He'd been offered a career position coordinating research efforts throughout the whole Horn of Africa (the northeastern bulge of the continent), including Sudan, Chad, Ethiopia, Eritrea, Djibouti, Somali, and upper Egypt. It was an incredible offer, abounding with honor for the job he'd done.

David had planned to attend Southwestern Baptist Seminary in Fort Worth before he took on any permanent position. His mentor, Lee, had gone to Southwestern. But the idea of "going career" right away was tempting; it would get him back out in the field that much quicker. But he was undecided and didn't want to rush what God might have for his future.

All of the countries in David's projected domain had significant Arab populations, but he would be based in an area that was primarily Orthodox Christian and Amharic-speaking. David wanted the job and the responsibility, but the prospect of learning another language and a different culture made his last two years feel wasted. David wanted to be based out of a city that was primarily Arab, like Khartoum, N'djamena, or even where he was already settled in Amman, Jordan. (There was, however, a distinct advantage to Ethiopia: David hadn't been kicked out of it yet.)

Our friendship continued to flourish, evidenced in part by the evolving subject matter of our e-mails: personal life outside of ministry. David had a younger brother, Danny, and a younger sister, Sara. His brother was twenty-three at the time and had just graduated from the University of Denver. He was studying for the MCAT tests with a view toward medical school. David used to joke, "Obviously, he's the one making the money in the family." And he wasn't getting kicked out of foreign countries either.

The small things were really starting to matter to me regarding David. I wanted to know about his family and his hopes for the future. I was starting to understand that for a deeper relationship to develop, we would probably have to actually see one another and get past the relatively safe buffer that e-mail provided. I had a lot to consider regarding this man and his future. I had felt called to the mission field since high school, and wasn't sure if marriage or a serious relationship was part of that calling or not. David may have seemed the perfect choice from the outside, but our ministries were very different.

Even though we both had a heart for Arab Muslims, my ministry was much more people-oriented in nature. I developed deep relationships and stayed in the same place, offering consistency and trust. David's ministry was more quick and intense, more task-oriented. He went into a situation, assessed it, and left the deeper relational work for a later team. In that way, we were very different, yet we both shared a deep call to life on the mission field. So I didn't know where our relationship was headed, or where David would be in the next few months. But of this I was sure: God's will would prevail.

Imagine my shock when the mother of the family where I was visiting my friend handed me the phone saying it was David McDonnall in Jordan calling me. As she did so, she had that motherly "why is this boy calling you?" look on her face. I took the phone sheepishly. We had never talked on the phone during our e-mail correspondence in the previous five months, and now I was standing in a stranger's home taking his call. My shock soon affected my body. I was so nervous and agitated, I could not get up from my seat because my legs no longer worked! I answered the phone doing my best to sound completely coy. "How did you figure out where I was?"

"I had to hunt you down. I had an old telephone number of your friend's, called it and found out she'd moved. I convinced the person living there that I was a good and upstanding boy and finagled the phone number from her."

I was impressed, to say the least. We talked briefly and he wished me an early Merry Christmas and safety as I traveled. We hung up, my heart began beating and legs working again, and I made my way out of the room before the questions and teasing began.

The following day we went to Bethany (located on the east side of Jerusalem) to pick up last minute gifts for our families back at home.

We left in the morning, so by the time we passed the Dome of the Rock in Jerusalem the sun was high and the air exceptionally clear. The sun reflected brightly off the Dome—the gold glare almost hurting our eyes as we commented on its brilliance that day. As I shopped in the marketplace, my mind wandered back to David, and I purchased him a genuine shepherd's slingshot. After all, shouldn't every David have a slingshot? I mailed it to him with Christmas greetings before I left. Later, David told me in an e-mail that he had taken a group of volunteers to Mt. Nebo that same day we crossed in front of the Dome of the Rock commenting on its brightness. They too saw the Dome that morning from Jordan, and were amazed at its brilliance as the golden Dome shimmered in the sun even from many miles away. I had to use David's supervisor's mailbox, so his supervisor picked up the package and delivered it to him. That required some explaining. Why was he getting a package from some girl in Israel? David just smiled and casually told him it was just from that Carrie Taylor, a fellow Journeyman across the river. From then on his supervisor referred to me as "That Carrie Taylor."

* * *

I was thrilled to be heading home to the States, back to Tex-Mex food and Dr. Pepper, for which I had found no Middle Eastern substitute. I was excited to see my family and have a normal American Christmas. But deep down, I was also thankful to leave the violence and Ramadan.

My friends and my new Arab family sent me away with flair: well wishes and gifts for my parents. I went home with liters of olive oil and olives, fresh from the harvest. I carried them with me on the plane so they wouldn't break, and by the time I got home my back ached from carrying heavy jars of Middle East delights halfway around the world. But arriving with these gifts was the most tangible way to demonstrate to my family the generous and hospitable nature of the Arab people.

Entering America had an entirely new meaning to me. At the Dallas-Fort Worth airport, under the sign that said, "Welcome to the United States of America," I nearly burst into tears. Though I loved the new friends I'd made and the intriguing land I had called home for two years, pride welled up in me as I passed under the sign and the star-spangled banner. I was home!

My heart was flooded with excitement at the prospect of my family being just minutes away instead of miles away. When the customs agent stamped my passport and kindly said "Welcome home," he had no idea how powerful those words were to me at that moment. Nor did my grinning "Thank you" convey what I really felt.

In addition to a bag with all the gifts from Israel, I was carrying another bag with enough necessities to get me by in case my checked luggage decided to take a world tour before arriving in Texas. At the baggage carousel, one bag appeared—the one filled with souvenirs and gifts: carpets, T-shirts, olive wood carvings, and Christmas ornaments. When my other bag failed to appear—the one with my clothes and personal items—I offered up a prayer that it would come out. My patience was being stretched as my family was just yards away on the other side of customs. No such luck. My other bag had taken a detour to Germany. After wading through the red tape associated with having it delivered to me, I made my way to the exit.

The disappointment over my luggage disappeared the moment I caught sight of my family—my mom and dad, sister Jen, and her two children. I couldn't hold back the tears any longer. I was home at last after eighteen months away.

Entering the States again felt a bit like stepping foot in a foreign country. I would fall into Arabic when talking about my experiences and have to backtrack and explain so people could understand. It was also strange going into a bookstore and seeing shelves of Christian books—right alongside shelves of books about Buddhism, New Age spirituality, and Islam. Suddenly, I felt more oppressed than when in Israel's Muslim population. I thought, "Why is the Baby being hidden in the very season that proclaims His coming?"

I thought about the joy I'd felt in Israel visiting the Sea of Galilee, the Mount of Olives, the Western Wall of the Temple, and Nazareth, and how lucky I was to have witnessed the places where Jesus walked. More than anything, it bothered me that America was so sheltered, so immune to the pain and suffering all over the world. It felt like no one cared.

Here are some things I definitely loved about being home: no roadside checks, no interrogations in customs, and no border patrols. If someone left a sack unattended at the grocery store, it was just groceries, not a bomb. I felt as free as a bird. But I never felt free of my concern for my second homeland. I was constantly tuned to the news about the violence in the West Bank. When I was in Israel, I knew what was true. In America, I didn't ever feel I was getting the whole story and I worried for my friends and fellow workers.

David celebrated Christmas preparing for his trip to Ethiopia. He and his friends took a trip to Wadi Rum, Jordan, a tourist spot with sandstone rock climbing; to Petra, an incredible site where the temple is carved into the rock walls; and to Aqaba on the shores of the Gulf of Aqaba. In order to show his friends the carvings at Petra close up, they paid for donkeys to take them to the highest elevations.

David and his friends had planned to camp under the stars—until the Jeep broke down leaving them stranded in the desert. David wrote,

I remember my life with David like this: close, happy, united in purpose.

Walking the walls of Jerusalem in 2000.

For nearly two years, I worked in this northern Israeli village.

I loved to sing and play my guitar and dulcimer for the children.

The front third of this modified shipping container was my home, sweet home for almost two years.

The grandparents and daughter of an Arab Druze family that "adopted" me while I lived in Israel.

Shopping in the open-air markets was a delight—fresh, unique food, sights, and sounds.

I spent two weeks participating in author Beth Moore's video project in Israel. Several years later we met again at a Dallas hospital.

Jerusalem was a couple of hours away from my village. One of my favorite places was the Garden of Gethsemane.

David fell in love with the Arab people and their culture.

David enjoying his favorite pastime during a visit to the States in 2001.

David and an Arab friend making coffee in Sudan.

I looked forward to having a family with David. He had so much love for children.

On a trip to Sudan, David went into a Kassala market with $450 and left with twenty-five Sudanese swords!

David visiting the Red Sea in 1999.

David had a cake made for the night he proposed. It said, "Will you marry me?" in English and "I love you" in Arabic.

David and I at Southwestern Baptist Seminary in October 2001.

As a Texas A&M Aggie, I wasn't about to get married without my Aggie cowgirl boots!

Walking down the aisle to the Fighting Texas Aggie
War Hymn—a surprise from David.

David and I camping with our friend, Chris, and our dachshund, Macy (perched
on Chris's four-wheeler).

David won the Kurds with his winsome ways and smile. I love seeing his wedding band—the symbol of how he won my heart as well.

Iraq does get cold in the winter, so my scarf kept out the cold and was handy to provide a customary head covering.

David spending time with new friends at an Iraqi market.

The Iraqi women are beautiful, strong, intelligent, and passionate. They provide the best for their families, even in times of war.

Wherever we went in the Middle East, children joined us as we walked—like at this marketplace in Sudan.

We celebrated our first anniversary with a picnic in Iraq—cake and all!

Customary long skirts are not ideal for wading into streams. I'm taking a picture of David at our anniversary picnic.

Our team that was attacked by terrorists in Mosul, sharing a meal at an Iraqi home. (l-r) Larry and Jean Elliott, Karen Watson, me, and David.

The glory of Saddam's earthly palaces (shown here) cannot compare to the glory my dear friends and husband are experiencing now in heaven.

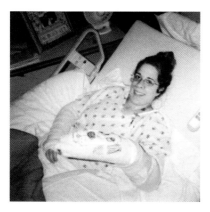

Parkland Hospital in Dallas, eight days after the attack. My friend, Rebekah, turned my cast into a work of art.

After climbing all over the Middle East, I couldn't imagine learning to walk again.

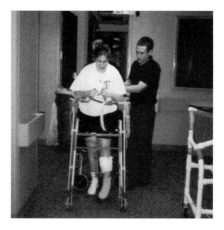

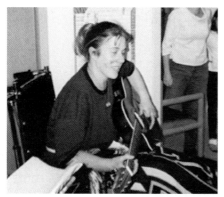

With one finger remaining on my left hand, I couldn't play my right-handed guitar, so the Ovation Guitars company sent me a brand new left-handed one!

My parents snuck my dog, Macy, into the hospital to see me.

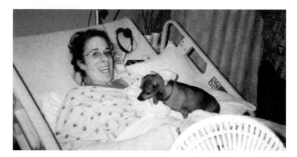

My only consolation in losing my husband and best friend is knowing he now worships in the presence of the One who laid down His life for us—Jesus Christ.

"This left myself, my roommate, and the three girls with us stranded about a mile and a half from the nearest road. So we instructed the girls to take only what was necessary for the night, along with water, flashlights, and our jackets. We locked up the rest of our stuff in our truck. I knew the road was straight west of us, so I checked my compass, picked out a landmark—more of a shadowy mountain as it was dark by now—and we began our hike out of the desert sand and finally reached the relative safety of the road. But it was still another 10 km to the resthouse where the others were waiting."

David's camping fiasco filled me with longing. No matter what he did, it always turned into an adventure. By contrast, I felt I was missing something in the comfort and security of my home in the United States. I wanted to be beneath the ancient temples, camping out under the stars, and yes, even finding my way out of the desert in the middle of the night. I knew I would probably never feel complete in either place. In the United States, I had my friends and family, but I had gained an extended family in Israel. I missed those relationships when in America—shopping in the Golan Heights with the girls, changing our path to town because Israeli helicopters, armed and facing north toward Lebanon, were blocking the necessary road. It may sound strange, but I missed the constant sense of "journey" that life in Israel represented. One never knew what to expect.

This was an important revelation to me. I didn't expect to miss Israel and the Middle East once I was back home in Texas—but I did. Nor did I expect to miss David and his can-do, what's-around-that-corner perspective on life as much as I did. These feelings made me realize that ministry to Arabs in the Middle East—the need, the unpredictability, the adventure, and the ability to trust in God's provision—had taken root in my heart. I wasn't sure what it meant, but I knew the feelings were real.

The rest of David's account about being stranded in the Wadi Rum national park will show you what I missed: "Having no other recourse, we turn towards the resthouse and continue our night trek/hike. Fortunately, we'd only been walking along the road for about twenty minutes when one of the cars in our caravan came looking for us. We piled in, rode back to the resthouse, and met up with the others. Again, I asked my roommate why I always seemed to attract trouble, but he said it made for an interesting two years."

The Journeymen group ended up in Aqaba in southern Jordan at the tip of the Gulf of Aqaba (across the border from Eilat where I had first spent extended time with David on our group's vacation), but their luggage, and the broken rental truck was still back in Petra, so the next day David drove back to the tourist site: "We loaded into this heavy-duty jeep and headed back to Rum on a rescue mission for the vehicle. This day turned into another fiasco, as these two guys (the Hertz representative, and the mechanic) tried everything they could to get the Jeep running again—all to no avail. We tried pulling out the Jeep with a Nissan truck but only succeeding in getting the Jeep's carburetor filled with sand. Then, we tried pulling it out with heavy-duty tow straps, which severely bent the Jeep's bumper. Finally, we gave up the idea of using the Jeep, and we went in search of a bigger truck to pull out the Nissan—which was supposed to be the rescue vehicle."

As I read David's words, I just laughed aloud. I knew if there was anyone who would enjoy the moment, regardless of the trouble at hand, it was he. Life couldn't get any better for David than to be broken down in the middle of an ancient national park in Jordan.

"We finally found a bedouin man who had a fifteen-ton Mercedes flatbed 4WD truck. It was HUGE! We hired the bedouin guy, and after several attempts we finally succeeded in getting the

Nissan out (and eventually the Jeep as well). However, since the transmission wasn't working—the wheels wouldn't turn, we literally 'drug' it out for nearly 3 km out of the desert. It was an all-day affair, but what else did we have to do?"

While David skittered from one desert adventure to the next, I'd caught a nasty cold and spent my holidays in a Nyquil stupor, watching the Aggie bowl game and babysitting my niece and nephew.

New Year's Day 2001 lacked the excitement of the previous millennium celebration in Bethlehem, but I sensed the year ahead would bring many changes. I had only five months left on my assignment in Israel, and David only two left on his in Jordan. Our futures were wide open, and neither of us had made any move to address what we thought about that in terms of our relationship. Clearly, his e-mails meant the world to me. My prayers were filled with constant requests for his ministry, and I desired to observe him in his leadership role someday. But I didn't allow myself to think of romance. David had showed no obvious interest in moving our relationship beyond where it was, and it appeared our lives would soon go in separate directions. At least, that's what I thought.

While I was still in the States on my Christmas break, David flew to Ethiopia to look into the career field operations position he had been offered by his supervisors. He and his good friend Joseph* traveled by train into the deeper parts of the country to meet with the person who would be David's permanent supervisor.

On the train in Ethiopia, he witnessed firsthand the smuggling of new stereo equipment, and took detailed notes on how the crime took place with the help of all generations of one family. On this long trip there was nothing to do other than watch the intricate smuggling operation. David watched and wrote in his journal: "Joseph's mother always said nothing good ever happens past midnight. This was clearly evident by the low-class, high-risk midnight smuggling operation we observed at various control stations in the country."

Ethiopia was a relatively easy country in which to travel. When stepping off the train in Bahir Dar, David got to play tourist in the beautiful lush green city on the shores of Lake Tana. He took a tour of the Blue Nile Falls, which are magnificent and the second largest in all of Africa. The guide's promised twenty-minute hike turned into an hour, even for an experienced hiker like David. But he found it worth the effort—the Blue Nile empties into the Nile and starts its long journey to the Mediterranean at the spectacular falls. I would have swapped my Texas congestion and cold for the Blue Nile Falls in a heartbeat.

David's journey took him by bus into Gondar, Ethiopia's former capital, which has a rich Christian history. Gondar was a saving grace for David, as he saw what life would be like if he took the permanent supervisor position he was considering. He would be completely immersed in the Amharic language instead of Arabic and completely removed from the Arab-Muslim populations that had been his focus up to this point. He asked several times if there were any Sudanese in the area but got blank stares in return. He soon learned that flights from Metameh, Ethiopia, to the Sudanese border had been halted due to violence. Because he was not conversant in Amharic, they could do little research. With each step farther away from the Sudanese population, David's desire for the permanent supervisor position for the Horn became less strong.

David spent time with the Lord on this trip considering his relationship with me and how he should handle it. It was during this time the Lord led him to be open and honest with me about his feelings and his desire to pursue a relationship beyond friendship.

David was nervous about revealing his heart but excited that the Lord had given him permission to do so. He still had two weeks before he would regain Internet access, so he spent the time writing a letter to me in his mind.

I completed my Christmas vacation with my family and returned to Israel. I hadn't received e-mails from him all the while he was in Ethiopia. It felt like an eternity. I prayed diligently for his safety and realized that I was becoming a person who cared a great deal about the well-being of one David McDonnall—and this was not just because he was a brother in Christ. My concerns for him were growing deeper all the time. There was an empty place getting bigger in my heart the longer I didn't know where he was and how he was doing.

When I finally received an e-mail telling me of his latest adventures, I savored every word. Reading his words was like taking gulps of cool, crystal-clear spring water after a hot day in the arid Israeli hills. I was relieved to hear from my friend and to know that he had arrived in Jordan safely. Then I received a second e-mail from him on the same day. I was overjoyed! What a treat! I hadn't even had time to reply to his first one.

But my stomach tightened as I read the subject line: "Honesty." What was this about? Was he going to tell me that we needed to be honest with each other and that he could no longer e-mail me for some reason or another? Or was he going to share honestly what he felt about me? His most recent e-mails provided no clues either way. I prayed and sat with my finger poised on the computer mouse, not knowing if I was ready to click my way into a David-less future.

I went through some self-talk before clicking: regardless of what anyone says to me, I am a child of the King . . . I will remain a child of the King . . . Christ will always be my first and One True Love. I was ready. I took a deep breath, clicked on "Open," and began to read, exhaling with relief the further down the page I scrolled. David was baring his heart to me, telling me how he felt about me and our relationship, making himself completely vulnerable—and doing it all without a clue as to how I would respond. Other than that I cared for him as a good friend, I had given him nothing more than my rapt attention when we were together.

He told me how he came to the decision to share his feelings towards me, his desire for us to date once we returned to the States, and how he had enjoyed getting to know me over the past few months. The bottom line was this: the ball was now in my court. It was my turn to open up and be honest with him. Unfortunately, I was out the door, getting an early start to spend the day in the Golan Heights with a friend! I certainly didn't have time to sit and pour my true feelings out in an impromptu e-mail. This would require writing, rewriting, editing! So I shut down my Internet account and left.

All day I wondered how I should respond. I probably made a lousy companion for my friend, since my mind was focused on composing the most perfect e-mail back to David.

We arrived home just as the sun was going down. I sat down at my computer and made an effort to put my feelings toward him into words. I told him that I, too, had enjoyed getting to know him, how I looked forward to hearing from him, how I loved how he could make me laugh—and how I like to laugh. I told him how the Lord had assured me that our relationship was a blessing and that I, too, looked forward to a time when we could begin dating in the States.

It's been said that writing makes you crystallize your thoughts—and it does. Words have meaning. There is a difference between saying "like," "love," "appreciate," or "admire"—especially in e-mail, where there is no body language, no tone of voice, no emotional color to give flavor to the stark words you are sending out. Which words to choose?

While I was composing my response, David was fretting. He didn't realize I'd been gone all day and later asked me why it took so long to write back. I laughed and explained what had happened and told him it was probably good that he had to sweat a little bit. He would have thought I was desperate if I'd written back immediately.

Though he sounded characteristically confident in his e-mail, I later learned that when my e-mail came to him he had his room-mate Chris, read the first few lines to see if it was good news or bad news. Chris told him he thought it sounded like a good reply, so David dove in and read the whole thing. He e-mailed me back, relieved that we were both on the same page.

Well, we were on the same page, but in two different countries. There really wasn't a whole lot that we could do to grow our relationship other than continue to write each other and make an occasional phone call. We were committed to honoring the Journeyman policy of team members not dating. We had started memorizing scripture together, keeping each other accountable each week for our verses and quizzing each other on old ones.

David had returned from Ethiopia thinking about his future and whether I was to be part of it. I called his surprise e-mail to me the DTR e-mail—Defining the Relationship. That was his goal and it was accomplished. We had committed to each other a mutual desire to pursue God's will concerning our relationship. That pursuit, however, could not move to the next level until our Journeyman terms were complete.

David's Journeyman service would end in March. Since most of his team would be leaving in June he decided to extend his term through the summer to help out during those months with different projects. So David went back to Colorado to visit his family before returning to Jordan to finish up his extended term. While he was there, we set up a time for me to call his parents' house in Colorado where he was staying. The time rolled around for me to call, and David was sticking close to the phone—casually, so he would be the one to pick up the phone. But at the time, his mother was in the room chatting with him, ironically enough, about when he might get married. She was nearest to the phone, and it became obvious that when I rang she would be the one to answer the phone.

I asked for David, but curiosity had the best of my future mother-in-law and she asked who I was.

"His friend, Carrie," I stumbled.

She passed David the phone but decided the room needed dusting and began cleaning the room. David hunkered down to try to muffle the phone and be nonchalant about the call. From my end, I knew something was up. David was rarely quiet, and even on an international call, I knew he was uncomfortable.

Later, he explained in an e-mail that his mother was standing close by. It's always so comical to me, how some situations can reduce us to an adolescent. Talking was never an issue for David, but on this day, in front of his mother asking about marriage, David was more than quiet.

But that phone call opened the door for David's mother. She now knew there was at least a possibility out there. I, however, staved off sharing anything about David to my family until I was back in the States.

CHAPTER TEN

Testing the Waters

Amman, Jordan—April 2001

While David was in Colorado, a friend and I began to plan a trip to Jordan before our term ended. Neither of us had yet had the opportunity to cross the Jordan River and see the sights on the other side. And of all the coincidences—"It just so happens that I have a friend living in Jordan (he's in Colorado right now but will be returning soon) who would love to show us around!" When David returned he cleared it with his supervisor to be in Jordan when we were planning our trip.

Liz* and I made plans for a place to stay and how we would travel to the border. David planned everything else like our personal travel agent. We agreed on an itinerary and waited for the day of our departure.

As the day approached for us to leave, I became increasingly nervous! I couldn't eat or sleep. I couldn't believe I was making the trek to Jordan—that was exciting enough. But if I allowed myself to think about the real reason I was so excited, it would only have made matters worse. Never in my life had I been this agitated! The night

119

before we left I would sleep . . . wake up . . . sleep . . . wake up—all night. While I waited on my friend to pick me up, I sent David a quick e-mail telling him I looked forward to seeing him and joked with him about not going to the wrong border crossing. We got to the border, completed our paperwork, and walked across the bridge as David suggested. We went through the gate on the opposite side and set foot in Jordan—but there was no David to meet us. There are so many variables at work in that part of the world that can impact schedules, so we didn't worry. We sat down and waited.

After an hour we tried my cell phone—thankfully it still worked since we were right on the border. We called his apartment—no answer. We called some of his teammates—no answer or they didn't know where he was. We called my friend's supervisor and told her of our predicament: stranded in Jordan. She promised to try to find someone who could locate David.

In the meantime, we had to decide whether we should stay or go—not back to Israel, but on to Amman, to the guesthouse where we were going to stay. After all, we were resourceful women; I knew enough Arabic to get us around town, though I had no idea how to get to the guesthouse or anything else about the city of Amman. But after a phone call, we learned what street it was near and the name of the neighborhood. So we grabbed our bags and got ready to hail a taxi. The first cab that came up was one that had already come by offering us a ride (but at an outrageous price). He stopped again and offered us a better price since we would be sharing it with another woman passenger.

The woman was already in the back seat, so that left one seat in the back and one in the front for us. My friend normally prefers the front seat because she gets motion sickness in cars when traveling—but this time she headed for the back seat. I had to violate Arab culture and ride in the front seat with the Arab driver. Though he did nothing to make me feel uncomfortable, I wanted to disappear. I had lived in the Arab culture for too long to be comfortable violating their standards of mixed company in public. An Arab woman would likely not have put herself in that situation but waited for another cab—and paid the higher price if necessary.

So there we were, barreling along at high speeds on a winding, two-hour trip to Amman. We tried to start up a conversation with our fellow traveler, a nun originally from Spain. She didn't know a lick of English, so she began ticking off the languages she knew: Spanish (all I remembered from high school was, *Donde esta el baño?*—Where is the bathroom?), Italian, Latin, French, and finally Arabic. Bingo! So she and I tried to carry on a conversation in Arabic. This was so typical of the multicultural Middle East: an American missionary and a Spanish nun conversing in Arabic while careening toward Amman, Jordan, in a cab.

We finally arrived in Amman, dropped our traveling companion at her destination and began trying to find our guesthouse. The driver didn't know where it was either, but was an expert at the time-honored tradition of asking directions from everyone we passed. We finally arrived, checked in, and called Liz's supervisor to let her know we were okay—but still without David. Ten minutes later we heard David's booming voice echoing in the stairwell, then a knock at our door.

All my nervousness over meeting David, long since forgotten with the day's adventures, returned in a wave that rushed over me. I was thankful to have Liz to run interference. She opened the door and welcomed a sweating, apologetic David.

As it turned out, we *had* gone to different border crossings. Israel and Jordan share three border crossings: one in the north, one in the middle close to Jericho, and one in the south near Eilat. I assumed he knew we would cross in the north (close to where I was staying). David assumed the middle border, close to where my friend lived because he knew she was driving us to the border. So the whole time we were waiting at the northern border, he was waiting south of us at the middle border. He began calling his teammates trying to see if anyone had heard from us but couldn't reach anyone. After waiting for six hours (he had gotten there extra early so as not to miss us!), he left and went to his apartment in Amman. He finally reached Liz's supervisor by phone, who told him we were proceeding to the guesthouse.

David is such a planner and executor of plans—and a "fixer" even when things go awry—that he felt terrible about our being left stranded. But it was an innocent mix-up and no harm was done. Liz and I were ready to enjoy our time in Jordan.

We freshened up and all three left to join Emily*, another mutual friend, for dinner. We ate at a nice restaurant that serves American style cuisine. David rightly assumed that I would appreciate the opportunity to enjoy some American food. It was a small thing, but it showed how considerate he was, how much he thought about others and anticipated their needs. I will never forget munching on real tortilla chips with artichoke-spinach dip. Divine! I suddenly realized that I'd eaten only nervously and sporadically for the two weeks previous in anticipation of meeting David. The American food brought back my appetite, and being with David allowed me finally to relax.

There was a lot riding on this meeting for David and me. This was the first time we'd seen each other since sending our DTR e-mails. Electronically, we had each staked out a bit of relational turf, and now it was time to talk face-to-face. That couldn't happen in a group of four, of course, and Liz carried the conversation over dinner. But both of us knew there was much to discuss as soon as we had the opportunity. David returned us to our guesthouse after dinner and promised to pick us up bright and early the next morning to begin a full day of sightseeing.

The next day we toured different areas around northern Jordan (Jerash, Ajilun, and Umm Qays). We saw crusader castles, Roman amphitheaters, and many other ancient ruins. You can almost throw a stone in any direction in the Middle East, the crossroads of ancient history, and hit something that has been there for centuries.

As we headed back toward Amman, we became lost as David wasn't completely familiar with that area of Jordan. But since "lost" is just a synonym for "adventure" to David, he took it all in stride. He began to share his heart with me while we tooled around on back roads trying to find our way home.

Not one to mince words, he went on about how "awesome" I was and how he had enjoyed getting to know me over recent months. While I appreciate David's sentiments, I was a little self-conscious with Liz in the back seat! She had woken up feeling sick that morning and had felt progressively worse as the day wore on, and I hoped she was actually asleep, not just resting, in the back seat.

David didn't seem to care who could hear him. He was pouring out his heart as if he would explode if he didn't tell me everything he'd been thinking. He reminded me of a hot can of Coke that had bounced around on the floorboard for hours over Jordan's rocky roads—pop the top and look out!

I wasn't sure who this awesome woman was he was describing—he was saying way more than I expected to hear, and I wasn't sure how to respond. I just sat quietly watching the road, taking it all in and pondering what in the world I should say in reply to his heartfelt confessions. When David finished up his "you're so awesome" speech (as we later named it), all I could come up with was a shy, over-whelmed, "Uh, thank you."

David pulled over in a small village to get us a cold soft drink and ask directions. He jumped out of the car seemingly oblivious to my inability to respond coherently to what he had been sharing. But there was someone who was not oblivious at all. I heard a groan from the back seat: "I think I'm going to be sick," she managed.

I asked if she wanted some Pepto-Bismol (second only to a pass-port in importance for foreigners), thinking she was referring to her stomach condition.

"Well, that too," she said. "But it's you two who are going to make me sick!" I laughed out loud, realizing she'd been awake during David's soliloquy.

In my defense, I turned around in the seat and said, "What do you say after that?!"

She paused, "Thank you was good . . . ." I felt better, knowing she understood my predicament.

We made it back to Amman around six o'clock, and David said he would return in an hour to take me out for dinner—our "unoffi-cial first date." I barely had enough time to jump in the shower to wash the dust off from the day's travels.

David had asked while I was in Israel if he could take me out to dinner. As I was packing, I had debated over what to wear, as any normal woman would. My only problem was that all of my nice clothes had turned to rags during my months in Israel. The bleach and ammonia that I worked with had ruined a number of shirts and pants, and what those chemicals didn't ruin, the hot desert sun did, beating its relentless heat upon my clothes as they hung out to dry.

In the summers, the sun is so hot and the air so dry that you can put your clothes out on one end of the line, work your way to the other end, and the first several items will be ready to be folded and put away. So for our first official dinner, my "Sunday best" looked worn and ragged. I definitely appeared to be the foster home dweller I was.

My choices were my nicest pair of khaki pants, a blue, button-down shirt with a white shirt under that (formally known as the "Blockbuster" uniform) or a summer dress with a hole in the back of it. I went with the pants. I figured with my luck, the hole would grow bigger that night, leaving me in a predicament I would rather not have to endure! I ironed and starched the khakis, hoping that the creases would hide their faded and worn look and make it appear as if I meant for them to look that way. I pulled my clothes out of my back pack, fluffing them out; looking in the mirror I decided, *not too bad,* the starch had held.

I curled my hair, added some makeup and a splash of perfume. All the while, my nerves grew more and more unsteady. I was very excited to finally have some time with David face to face, but I was nervous. His previous conversation did nothing to allay my fears. *What if he thought I was different than my e-mails? What if he was different? What if he was a total dork? I would be stuck with him for the rest of the evening by myself, without Liz there to bail me out!*

So far he didn't seem to be that way, but maybe he was holding out on me. *What if…?* I finally scolded myself. I could go on all night with the "what ifs." The fact remained that I liked David or at least what I knew of him in his e-mails. I was very much looking forward to this night, and worrying about things either way would do me no good.

David arrived an hour and a half later, a little later than he had said. That was *totally* fine with me, as I was running behind (which is not unusual for me).

He knocked on the door and Liz yelled out a taunting "He's here...."

I took one more glance in the mirror. *Makeup—good. Hair—good as it is gonna get. Lipstick—straight, none on the teeth. Clothes—well, they're there too.* I said a quick Nehemiah prayer—*Father, help me*—and walked casually down the hall, trying my best to hide my nervousness and excitement. I came around the corner. There was David, and *he looked good*! He was holding a bouquet of flowers and smiling from ear to ear. I took the flowers, said thank you, and quickly put them into some water. At that moment, I realized this was the first time a date had ever brought me flowers.

As we walked out the door I checked out his attire; he was wearing black Wranglers, a button-down shirt, and a suede vest—with boots, of course. He had returned to the States a few weeks prior and brought this clothing back with him, knowing I was coming to Jordan. Once in the car, David prayed for our time together. We started off to our first destination. He began explaining that we had arrived back in Amman later than he'd hoped—he had planned to take me to the Citadel in time for the Muslim evening prayer call at sundown. Standing as it does on top of the hill nestled alongside several others, the call to prayer echoes throughout the valley, as they all start up at different times, creating a round of calls. The sound is ominous and is accompanied by a flicker of green light that shines from the top of the *minarets* (prayer towers). David had hoped to bring me there at to watch the sunset, experience the call from that particular spot, and to pray over the city. But we'd missed sundown due to our late return.

Even though it was dark, David took me to the Citadel. He said it was still a nice sight and would be lighted. We arrived and the guard quickly informed us that the park was closed. David expressed his disappointment, and as he walked back to get into the car, the guard said, "But since you came...."

A man who claimed to be a tour guide there escorted us through the park, telling David of the sights while I hung back listening and looking around. Jordan is an amazing country with many historical locations. I marveled at the wonder of it all, when all of a sudden the man escorting us took off like a shot, whispering, "The police! The police!"

David started running after him. I supposed he'd had too many close calls with the international police force to want another. I walked faster, not wanting to run through the rocky terrain in my cheap sandals. After all, I really didn't see what the problem was, we were invited in.

Once back at the car, we bid our adieus and thanks to our escort. As we pulled out of the parking lot, David explained that the "tourist police" were walking the grounds, and the guard could have gotten into a lot of trouble for leading us in after hours. I was unmoved by his fear. Granted, I knew he'd been detained more than his fair share of instances, but me running in bad sandals over the rocks? It wasn't going to happen. I thought the whole thing was hilarious, but David wasn't laughing as yet. He was thankful to have "escaped." We left our little escapade for the restaurant. David seemed a bit distracted as he drove, saying that he was not used to driving in the city. He didn't own a car and generally took taxis or had a team supervisor drive him. So after circling the same streets a few times, I was starting to get annoyed.

It became evident that he was unsure which restaurant he wanted to visit, and I remember thinking how very disorganized he was for not knowing. He finally pulled up to one, claiming he didn't remember exactly where it was, but this was it. We walked into a smoke-filled restaurant, and as the hazy cloud parted we entered. All faces turned to greet us. All of them male.

I quickly assessed that I was the *only* woman in the room, except for the hostess. She came quickly and politely suggested that perhaps we would like another restaurant with much better food, atmosphere, etc. This was a men-only bar.

We turned and hastened from the restaurant. David was embarrassed and told me that it had been a great family restaurant just a few weeks prior. Well, not so much now! He led me around the corner to try another restaurant, but on the way to it we came across a French restaurant. It had a maître d' on the street level who escorted us in an elevator up to the restaurant.

The room was lit by the soft glow of candlelight, classical music filled the air, and a waiter in a tux showed us to our table. We sat at a table for two draped with soft white linen, overlooking the city. We were the only people there so the service was wonderful. We glanced over the menu, neither one of us having a clue about French cuisine. If we'd been in the Sudan, ordering goat intestines, we would have been covered. I ordered chicken-something—I figured it was pretty hard to mess up chicken. We had a wonderful and romantic time. I later learned the mix-up over the restaurant was because I'd dressed so shabby (remember, all I had). David had planned to take me to a really nice restaurant, but when he saw my casual and worn look, he abruptly changed his plans without hurting my feelings.

The following day was the big trip down to Petra, and we would need an early start to get there, tour the grounds, and return to Amman all in one day. At some point during the night Liz got really sick. She called David around three in the morning to see if he had any medicine, and he came over with his Third World, lost-in-the-desert emergency first aid kit. After Liz was medicated, he left to get a few more hours of sleep before he returned to pick us up to go to Petra. I slept peacefully through the whole ordeal.

I awoke the next morning to find Liz resting on the couch, medicine strewn across the coffee table, evidence of her fitful night. She was blanched and exhausted, not up for the long ride to Petra. So when David returned two hours later, he and I left alone. The long drive gave us plenty of opportunity to get to know one another better.

Unfortunately, I am *not* a morning person; this was only made worse by the early rise. Fortunately, we stopped for a donut and coffee as we left the city. Coffee helps, but I'm still a long way from perky as the sun rises. I joined in the conversation and slowly woke up. As we traveled across the desert, David shared stories of his journeys across North Africa. I regaled him with life in my village nestled on the side of a mountain in Galilee.

We moved on to college days, how we got to where we were, our families, our friends, music, embarrassing moments, and everything else that crossed our minds. As our conversation flowed, every now and then a moment of silence would fall.

Having been in the Arab world for almost two years, I had learned to adapt to their culture in several ways. One way was the moment of silence. I dare not generalize this to fit all across the Arab world, but only in the context of those whom I knew. This moment of silence is the same as we have in America, the kind when a conversation is going strong and then all of a sudden, almost unpredictably, it lulls into silence. Some people joke that that is when every person in the room is thinking about Abraham Lincoln. The biggest difference between the two is that Americans cannot handle the silence for very long. Most of the time, someone starts up the conversation again with a new topic, or if a new topic cannot be found, everyone laughs at the awkwardness of the moment and the silence is filled by small-talk. But for the part of the world that I lived in, this quietude could be left alone for several minutes at a time and linger in the air with ease.

I had often watched in amazement as a conversation that was going strong dwindles into silence and was left undisturbed by all those in its presence. A few times I had tried to pick it up, but was only met by silence. Everyone would just sit comfortably, silently contemplating the conversation. As the Amcrican, I would fidget uncomfortably wanting to break the quiet, but now due to my previous experience, I had learned to sit silently like a repentant child.

As David and I talked, these silences came naturally; I was almost unaware of them at first. Then I noticed more and more that David was unusually uncomfortable with them, so instead of starting up the conversation, I began to play a game (unbeknownst to him). I would quickly glance at my watch and sit silently, waiting to see how long he could stand it. It was never very long before David would start in with a new story, leaving me laughing inside at his inability to handle the quiet. Later, when we were in the States, I confessed this game I had played. He laughed, knowing that he couldn't stand the silence, and then looked to the bright side. "I'm sure that's why my Arabic progressed faster," he said.

We arrived in Petra and David paid my way into the park. Petra is a place with which most Americans are familiar—if not from *National Geographic* or television travelogues, at least from the movie *Indiana Jones and the Last Crusade*. It's an ancient city carved out of vertical, red sandstone walls—the Sedona, Arizona of the Middle East.

We walked down the *sic*, a narrow canyon-floor pathway cutting through the three-hundred-foot rock walls. It's a wonder of nature that leaves you literally in awe of the creation of our Lord's hand. As you come out of the narrow pathway, the Treasury (the columned facade often seen in pictures) looms in front of you, huge and magnificent. There are several tall and impressive tombs and other fronts carved into the walls, which is why it's called the Street of Facades.

David began to escort me around this playground that the ancients left behind. He'd been there many times and so made an excellent tour guide. He took me to the base of the steps that led forever up to the top of Petra, "the high place."

We climbed 700 steps to the top where we found a perfectly flat surface in the rock. Here, the ancients came to make sacrifices, to appease a small, deaf god. Besides the history of this particular spot, it offers an incredible view of the majesty of the desert of Jordan. Jordan has been called the Switzerland of the Middle East, and it's easy to see why when one stands at the highest point and surveys the rocky crags below and the desert beyond.

While at the top, I realized I was as fascinated by David as I was the terrain. I had never met anyone with such energy—such a zeal for life! My nervousness about meeting him face to face was being replaced by nervousness that he might be the one! The more we got to know each other, the more we found out we were alike—same interests, same desires, and yet different enough to keep things interesting. What an amazing discovery I made on the top of a sacrificial rock in the mountains of Jordan.

After our tour we stopped for dinner at a local pizza restaurant in Petra. The owners and waiters all knew David by name and greeted him like a long-lost brother. They were complaining about how long it had been since they'd seen him. This was something I quickly noticed in all the places we went. Everyone knew David; everyone was excited to see him. Although warm greetings and hospitality are characteristic of the Middle East, this seemed more than culture—people always seemed genuinely happy to see him. This spoke volumes to me. People don't usually welcome those for whom they don't have high regard. Seeing the high esteem in which others held David raised my own estimation of his character.

We took a different route back to Amman, a highway that took us closer to the border of Iraq. We talked a little about that country and all the stories we had heard about what goes on in its secretive world. I remember thinking, "I guess that's one place I will never know about."

How wrong I was. I wonder now if God in heaven was looking down at two of His young servants falling in love, searching for the future, committed to serving Him, driving by a country they thought they'd never see. Unlike God, we can't see the beginning and the end at the same time. If we could, we might turn back. Since we can't, we trust that He can, and follow Him where He leads.

CHAPTER ELEVEN

David's Leadership Firsthand

Kassala, Sudan—July 2001

During my stay in Jordan, we had watched some videos from David's visits to Sudan. David's love for the Sudanese Arabs came shining through on the tapes, and his enthusiasm was contagious. I immediately felt God leading me to pray for the opportunity to make a trip into Sudan. Later that same evening, David told me of the need for a female translator to accompany his team on an upcoming trip. I prayed, and searched for the financial support to go on the trip, and a man in my mother's Sunday school class offered to fund it. I was on my way to Eritrea. I was thankful to at least be going to a neighboring African country. But I was humbled when God answered my prayer: at the last minute the trip got changed—to Sudan!

More and more I felt drawn to David (and he to me). I began to wonder if his adventure-filled life was one that I could embrace. So when the opportunity came to tour the Sudan, with David as the team's leader, I was ecstatic. I would be able to observe him in his element—see him as a shepherd and leader of a team of people who were depending on him. I also wanted to see if the Sudan was a ministry I could handle. I just wanted to know if this man and this country were what the future held for me. So I prayed about it diligently. In mid-July, our team left for Kassala in eastern Sudan, on the border of Ethiopia.

We arrived in Khartoum, the capital, and I could see David's countenance change. "Man, I love this country!" he said. "I'm grateful because the only way someone would ever love this place is if God was calling him here. Only God can impart such a love in one's heart for such an unlovable place."

My eyes were wide open at all the sights. Yes, it was an Arab nation, but also fully African—and the colors were brilliant. The sky radiated blue and the market was a kaleidoscope of color. There seemed to be as many camels as people, as if we were on the set of *Lawrence of Arabia*.

Our first evening in Khartoum, we went to Omdurman to see the whirling dervishes, an order of mystical Muslims who twirl and chant, spinning feverishly as part of their worship to Allah. The *Darwiish* (Dervish) are Sufi Muslims who want a close, personal relationship to God. In Omdurman, they meet in a cemetery at the grave of a Sufi who they believe could heal diseases. As they gather, they begin to chant the name of God in Arabic, rocking forward: "Allah, Allah, Allah, Allah," over and over, rhythmically and repetitively. As the evening progresses, they repeat the Islamic *Shahada*, their confession of faith, the first pillar of Islam: "*La ilah illa Allah*"—"There is no god but Allah." This is repeated over and over and over, faster and faster, bodies rocking back and forth while some in the center of the group spin round and round, whirling themselves into a near frenzy.

The scent of incense wafted over us, mixed with the smell of dust stirred up by the dervishes. My heart broke for the lost people of

Sudan, trying to find God by spinning and chanting. I looked at David and joined my tears with his. He'd seen the dervishes many times before, but the dark and demonic display we were watching sickened his stomach. We stood as a team, outside the ring of spectators watching the dervishes, and prayed and sobbed and begged God for mercy on the nation.

The fact that the ceremony was taking place in a cemetery was a clear reminder of the need for life after death. David wondered how people could be so surrounded by the evidence of death and still ignore the eternal life God offered. He prayed that he'd never get comfortable with the "lostness" of those without Christ. He asked God for a deep passion to burn within him to do something, whatever he could, to alleviate the suffering in Sudan.

After that night, David was ready to sign on the dotted line to spend his life in Sudan. As I watched him, it was clear his intensity knew no bounds. A life with David McDonnall would never be a life lived halfway—ever. This man was pedal to the metal, all or nothing.

David and I sat on the bus together as we rode to Kassala, his favorite town in the entire country. This was the first chance we'd had to talk on our trip. David was being cautious about our relationship since we were both desirous of abiding by the Journeyman policy of staff not dating. Besides, we were in an Arab culture where close male-female relationships in public were not common. David had been so consumed with organizing and leading our trip that he had paid little attention to me, to the point that I wondered if he was having second thoughts. But our time on the bus calmed my fears. It was the first time he hadn't been consumed with other things and we were able to talk.

But apparently we hadn't been completely discreet. The previous night in the hotel, group leader Tony* had taken David to task about our relationship. David later said, "He held my feet to the fire and asked me tough, hard questions over this. I love him for it. He's a godly, godly man and I greatly appreciated his counsel."

Tony asked David if he thought I was the one. David had several fears about getting involved with me, even though in nearly every way we were compatible, from callings to spiritual walk, even to personality and hobbies. He claimed I was everything he wanted in a girl, but since we barely knew one another in person, he hadn't had time to become totally sure. And it was so much easier to focus on the ministry. He'd been asked to take a major job in the organization and that's where he chose to put his energy.

This is where Tony changed the course of our lives. He told David in a long and detailed monologue that we all have our own faults, and that none of us is perfect. Therefore, no matter how well David got to know me, we were still going to have personality differences and subtle conflicts. Tony reminded David that God loves us unconditionally and that's what he wants from us—to love others the same way He loves us.

David didn't shy away as a result of that conversation. In fact, it seemed to give him greater confidence and conviction. His focus on our trip was still on leading the team, not on me. But I was fine with that. I loved seeing David in this role. He was born to lead, and that really filled me with even greater respect for him. As we talked on the bus, my heart warmed for who David was and what he wanted to accomplish with his life.

We arrived in Kassala after eight hours on the bus—dirty, tired, and still needing to ride one more bus into the central part of town to the hotel. The Kassala region had been the site of a vicious battle that anti-government forces launched from the neighboring country of Eritrea in 1998. The land is parched and treeless, and three months after we left, Kassala was recaptured by government forces. The town is predominantly *Beja* people. It was stable but tense when we arrived, and as outsiders we were met with many questioning stares. Our team was massive by mission standards—thirteen in all—so we attracted no small amount of attention wherever we went.

After checking into our hotel, we dined at David's favorite Sudanese restaurant, an open-air café along the dirt streets of Kassala. With enthusiasm, he devoured the *salaat, kibde,* and *fasoulya*. However, the rest of the group, made up mostly of Americans, didn't share their leader's zeal for grilled hunks of lamb and chopped goat liver.

On our first full day in town, we had a prayer walk down the streets of town asking for God's mercy for the people. Since our guide was Muslim, David's job consisted primarily of keeping him away from the rest of the group as we prayed. It was early morning, and the *souq*, or open-air market, wasn't open yet, and the quiet allowed us to focus on our surroundings and prayer. The following day we did the same thing, but this time the Muslim guide let the "crazy *Khawajas*" (foreigners) walk around town and murmur by themselves. Later, we checked out the irrigation canal and a nearby mosque, which is all the town really had to offer. I knew we were in a foreign world when the irrigation canal was considered a major tourist attraction.

That evening was the first time I saw David upset. David was always in his element with people, but on this particular night, things had not gone well. First, he took our guide's advice on a restaurant, and the rest of us soon found out that if there's anything that can cast a cloud over David's normally cheerful demeanor, it's a lack of a suitable place to eat.

The restaurant was out in the open air in the desert heat without the benefit of trees or greenery to cool it down. The humidity was suffocating. Then there were the *bugs!* The lights around the table were magnets for the malaria-carrying mosquitoes and other annoying insects. We batted away the buzzing infiltrators that were trying to make a meal out of us as we waited longer and longer for our own meal to arrive.

It took over half an hour just to get bottles of pure water, and I could see David getting nervous. Not that he minded waiting, but the decision for where to have dinner had been his and he felt responsible for everyone's growing discomfort. After two hours we still had no food and only shallow promises of, "Five minutes more!"

Finally, David got up and walked to the kitchen and politely, but firmly, requested that whatever food they had ready be brought to the table. Unfortunately, they listened to him, and soon our table was covered with raw meat. While this was a great way to test our parasite prevention medicine, nobody was that hungry—not even after two hours of waiting. Chewing on a piece of raw goat meat in a Third World African country was asking for trouble, and everyone at the table looked to David for guidance. He shined his flashlight on the slimy pink matter, and then he cut into it with his pocketknife.

"David won't even eat it!" someone exclaimed, and we all laughed. But none of us dared eat it either.

To add insult to injury, the bill for this "feast" cost us nearly forty U.S. dollars, a fortune in Sudan. Later, as I listened to David rant and rave, I couldn't help but giggle. When he'd been abandoned in the desert at night with a broken-down truck, he didn't show this much emotion. David was such a perfectionist about his leadership role that his inability to control the meal situation pushed him to the limit. *Okay, so he went a little over the top with the control thing,* I thought. *No one's perfect.* But watching him, and seeing his standards, made me realize David would always take care of me to the best of his ability in any situation, and my trust in him deepened.

After a few more days of intense prayer and needs assessment, David was given the honor of purchasing traditional *Beja* swords for the team members and their families back home. He took his duties seriously and made a chart of the available monies and the cost of swords depending on their quality. He left for the *souq* with a pocket full of cash and a handwritten shopping list. If ever he was in his element, it was bartering in an open-air market. It was the American equivalent of buying a used car and coming out on top, and that was his goal that day.

While the women went looking for *jabanai* (coffee) pots, beads, and other crafts of the area, David led the men to the sword-buying area. "Gentlemen," David said, "let the buying proceed."

As David examined the first sword, a circle of salesmen formed around him. They were like bees drawn to flowers. It would have been worse if they had known that every pocket on his Cabela bush shirt and safari pants were stuffed with hundreds of thousands of Sudanese pounds.

Over the next three hours, the sword *souq* became the hot spot in town. When word spread that a *Khawaja* was buying up all the *Beja* swords in Kassala, things got intense. As the bidding and bargaining went forward, David's pockets grew lighter and the black bag at his feet grew heavier. By the time he shelled out the last Sudanese pound he had collected twenty-five traditional *Beja* swords. "*Yaa Salaam!*" he yelled. "That's a new record." (The previous record was twelve bought at one time.) It provided great Sudanese souvenirs for the team and a huge infusion of cash into the local economy.

The team members greatly appreciated David's skill in negotiating the good prices, but he thought they had done him the favor by turning him loose in the market with money to spend. He loved the frenzy, inspecting the swords, talking to the craftsmen. He didn't come away with a sword of his own, but thought he had gotten more than anyone. To thank him for his efforts, the team took up a collection to allow David to buy his own sword. Tony, our group leader, lured him back to the *souq* on the pretense of getting some tassels for his own sword.

David returned to the *souq* and announced, "*Asallaam alekum!*" (Peace be upon you all!). Again, the salesmen converged, carrying swords and daggers. Then Tony announced to David they were there to get David the sword of his choice. He was overwhelmed with the group's gift to him, and picked out a beautiful sword. He even asked the craftsman if he could put a silver handle on it and followed him back to his shop to make the change.

Walking back to the hotel, David might as well have been Sudanese himself. Sword in hand, kicking up dust in the street, admiring the brightly-colored robes of the *Beja* women, looking at the *Beja* men sipping tea congenially in the outdoor cafes, listening to the butchers shouting out prices for goat meat hanging in their stalls, inspecting the fresh fruit—David was at home in Sudan.

I fell in love with David in Kassala. Seeing him in a place he loved, in a ministry he was born for, helping people he admired—it all came together in this out-of-the-way town in the Horn of Africa. I realized now that our relationship was bigger than an e-mail chat. I wanted to spend time with him, to discover even more about who he was. And I also knew, if need be, I could live in the Sudan. While I, on my first visit, had not developed the same emotional intensity about the country as David had after numerous visits, I knew that would come with time. Our hearts broke the same way over the spiritual needs of the people, and I knew that if God led David there and me with him, I could make it my home. If Sudan was going to be David's world, and God wanted me to be with David, I knew I could make it mine as well.

CHAPTER TWELVE

My Time in the Middle East Ends

Southwestern Baptist Seminary, Fort Worth, Texas—September 2001

I returned to Texas after my Journeyman tour was up, and David followed near the end of the summer. We were both enrolled in seminary and living in Fort Worth. We were closer now than we had ever been and free to pursue our relationship.

Having seen David's competence in the African bush—about as far from a classroom as one could get—I wondered about his motives for attending seminary. I wondered if he might incline toward becoming a pastor. The last thing I saw in my future was being the wife of a pastor. I did not think of the pastorate as a lesser calling—I just knew beyond a shadow of a doubt that I was called to be a missionary. It would have been disobedient for me to have fallen in love with a man who was not also called to the mission field. I didn't want to rush things if it meant a lifetime of doing what I wasn't called to do.

"I'm not going to be a pastor," David assured me. "To me, the Christian life is an adventure—an experience—an experience with God. You have to constantly be seeking Him, allowing Him to guide the footsteps of your life. So right now, my experience with God is attending seminary in east Fort Worth."

It was a very hard time for us. Our good friend and fellow Journeyman co-worker, Genessa Wells, had been killed in Egypt when her bus struck a truck that was parked in the middle of the road. We were devastated at the news. Genessa was fun-loving, had a great laugh, was wonderfully-gifted and a devoted servant of the Father. And she wouldn't be coming back to her earthly home. She wouldn't be singing or laughing anymore in this life, though we knew she would be singing before the Lord. While we rejoiced in this, we were still left with the void her absence created in our network of dear friends.

And the news just got worse. The next day was September 11, 2001. New York and Washington DC were struck a devastating blow, as was our entire country. Nineteen Arab terrorists hijacked airplanes and crashed them into the twin towers of New York's World Trade Center and the Pentagon in Washington. Only a brave group of passengers, who sacrificed their lives in the sky over Pennsylvania, kept a third plane from being crashed into yet another site. David and his classmates gathered around a television and watched the World Trade Center towers fall.

The seminary cancelled services the next day and gathered to pray for the country. In a chapel service the seminary president said, "The time is too short, and the times too turbulent, for business as usual." Neither David nor I realized just how the global war on terrorism, ignited by the attack on the United States, would soon affect our lives.

David and I watched as Islamic extremist groups and Osama bin Laden were thrust into the spotlight. Arabs and Muslims in general were looked at with suspicion. Those of us with a deep love for the

Middle East and its people experienced a collage of emotions: disbelief, shock, grief, patriotic pride, and even anger. We knew God was sovereign and that He hadn't been surprised by Genessa's death, nor had He been caught sleeping on the morning of September 11. But we felt lost, and were disheartened. Being in the middle of America, we suddenly felt useless—as if we were in some great holding pattern and not moving forward for God.

We clung to this verse: "Therefore we do not lose heart. Though outwardly we are wasting away, yet inwardly we are being renewed day by day. For our light and momentary troubles are achieving for us an eternal glory that far outweighs them all. So we fix our eyes not on what is seen, but on what is unseen. For what is seen is temporary, but what is unseen is eternal" (2 Corinthians 4:16–18 NIV).

It was such an odd time to have a romance. David and I were falling in love in the midst of war, terrorism and lost friends. We continued to grow a single heart for the people of the Muslim faith. We were deeply concerned about the world's sentiment towards Muslims, and felt the pull to go back where we might do some good.

On September 18, a mere week after 9/11, David and I attended a fund-raising banquet for a ministry to Arab Muslims. We listened to powerful testimony from a Nigerian woman, a lifelong Muslim who had asked Jesus into her heart. Another Christian woman, married to a Muslim man, talked about living out her faith from deep within a Muslim home.

Those testimonies really started to resonate within David and me. This organization was run by Arab Christians, and we really wanted to be a part of that world again. September 11 only served to stir our hearts for how great the needs were in the Middle East. We prayed daily for the ministries working with Arab Muslims, and my own heart was crying out for those lost in the Arab world. While our country prepared for battle, so did we, but in a different way. Our love for the Arab Muslim world was only growing stronger.

Our year-long e-mail romance was finally being played out in the real world. We were close enough geographically—in the same metropolitan area—to begin spending time together on a regular basis. David wanted to kick off our relationship in the "real world" with a real first date. Granted, we'd had dinner in Jordan, but somehow getting kicked out of the Citadel park didn't have the romantic ring we were looking for.

The first "official" date consisted of a movie and a visit to the water gardens in downtown Fort Worth. But it was meeting my parents in the middle of September that caused David to panic. I've never seen him so nervous. Keep in mind that David, with his boisterous personality, didn't understand the meaning of the word *shy*. He was an extrovert through and through, but when he met my parents, I thought he might faint from panic. He was white as a sheet. He tried to think of it as a politician's moment: "This was just another instance of kissing babies and shaking hands."

He sat up straight in his chair, almost as if he touched anything, it might break. My parents tried to put him at ease, but I have to admit I was a bit gleeful watching him squirm. To think, this man who could walk into darkest Africa and barter for beads or fish, or join a dance in the midst of Israel, and was nervous meeting *my* parents? Well, it was a compliment.

Granted, I did spring the whole family on him: my mother, my father, my sister Jennifer, my niece, my nephew, but I hadn't expected David, the poster boy for calm in crisis, to have trouble with them. Little did I know that he was preparing to have "the talk" with my father, Jon Taylor. So later I found out why he'd been so nervous.

"I'd like permission to date your daughter," David said to my dad. My father knew that I was as hard-headed as they come, and he was taken aback and flustered, but he was honored by the question.

"Aw, shoot, yeah," my dad told him in his warm Texas drawl. "That's fine with me. You didn't have to ask me. I appreciate you asking, but you didn't have to."

My dad told David I had always had high moral standards for the guys I dated, and if David was good enough for me, then that was enough confirmation for him. After David received my father's blessing to pursue our relationship, he returned to his naturally extroverted self—and my family proceeded to make him feel included by telling him embarrassing stories from my past. The ritual was complete.

After that date, I think David was more uncertain of himself and us than ever. I mean, how long was it socially acceptable to date, and what was the next step for us? It was clear we were getting closer, but he was praying for neutrality in discerning God's will—even if it meant breaking up with me. David's first love was always the Lord and His calling, and I knew that—and was fine with it. My first love was the same. So I waited patiently for him to discover and become comfortable with God's will. In the meantime, we continued to see each other and ignore the elephant in the room.

September 11 continued to wreak havoc on the country, and extremist Muslims continued to be the target of America's retaliation. David and I had firsthand knowledge of the difference between extremists and the gentle souls locked within the dark world of the Middle East, but most of America did not. Our hearts truly grieved for what we heard from usually responsible Americans.

The end of September brought Genessa's funeral, and our group of Journeymen from the "Journeymen refugee camp" at Southwestern

Seminary rode four hours to Houston for her combined funeral and memorial service. David sang us a Ray Stevens medley the entire route, and Chris and I laughed uproariously at David's entertaining.

The funeral itself was inspiring. A crowd of more than 200 people packed the funeral home chapel—it was standing-room only when we arrived. There were so many testimonies about Genessa's life: high school and college friends, fellow Journeymen, career missionaries—all testified as to the impact she had on their lives and the world.

The testimonies at the funeral jarred us back into reality: individual lives do make a difference. In her final few minutes on earth, Genessa had been sharing Christ with people on the bus. She died fulfilling Christ's Great Commission to take the gospel into the entire world. The service ended with her high school friends singing MercyMe's song, "I Can Only Imagine," a song that talks about what it will be like to stand in the presence of the Lord for the first time.

David wrote this after the funeral: "I pray that at my funeral, people would be able to say half the things they testified at Genessa's funeral. I pray that my life is filled with that same, apostolic passion."

It was odd to celebrate the end of Genessa's life and be celebrating the possibility of our lives together at the same time. But her life certainly gave us hope about the potential for good that service for Christ holds, and we were eager to discover how that would be fulfilled in our lives—separately or together.

After the funeral, David and I went on a visit through College Station, Texas, where my alma mater, Texas A&M University, is located. It had been nearly two years since I had been on campus and I was really excited to show David a place that had been such an important part of my life. I was taking the man I loved to a place I loved. I introduced him to the whole "Aggie" culture, which is contagious. And though David teased me mercilessly, I think he loved hearing about my history there.

In touring the campus we came to an old oak tree that grew over the sidewalk. The tradition was that if you walked beneath a particular large branch with a sweetheart, you would marry that person. I hesitated as we got close to the tree, and I noticed David paused a bit as well. But we proceeded hand-in-hand towards the branch, and David pulled me close. "Well, here's hoping the tradition comes true," he said, as we walked together under the branch.

By the middle of October, David was anxious to show me more of his world, and I left for his hometown, Lamar, Colorado, for an antelope hunting trip. Looking back, I think this was my final test. Could I withstand a weekend in the wilderness with his family?

We flew to Amarillo where we were met by David's good friend from college, Dave Hale. Like all of David's other college friends, Dave Hale was married. The evening's dinner was like a who's-who of David's married friends. We ate dinner with Dave and Heather Hale (and their baby); Gary and Regina Bryant (and their baby); John and Amy Taylor (and Amy's pregnant belly). It felt odd to be the sole single couple at the table, but I felt like David was proudly showing me off. I was, of course, regaled with stories of David's college years, probably hearing more than he would have preferred. But that's what good friends do—paint the worst possible picture for the girlfriend-in-waiting.

In turn, he told stories of his time in Jordan and Africa that made life in Texas seem tame by comparison. I was proud to be sharing David with his friends, and know that I was there to witness firsthand some of what he described to the group. I know they were impressed at the depth of David's commitment to ministering to others in a needy part of the world.

After our cozy dinner in Amarillo, we headed to Lamar. It was my turn to "meet the parents." This is where my exhaustion worked for me. When we walked into David's childhood home, we'd been traveling for about ten hours, with only four hours' sleep the night before. So I was far too tired to be nervous. When I walked in and met David's mother, Donna McDonnall, I immediately was drawn to her warmth. They were a strong Christian family, and David's parents had hoped their legacy would continue in their kids.

David later told me how his mother had gotten dressed up for my arrival. She did look beautiful, and I was humbled at the trouble she went to for my arrival. It said a lot about the way she felt about David. The comfort I felt with his family was just another thing that drew me closer to David.

The one thing that might have stopped David from traveling around the world was his love of the Colorado outdoors. Giving up the familiar landscape of the mountains and the adrenaline of antelope hunting had been a true sacrifice for him. I really understood what the Lord meant to him on this trip. David would have given all to follow Jesus, and I had no idea how much David's beloved Colorado meant to him until I was there, sharing it with him. As I drifted off to sleep in his parent's house that night, I was certain that *this* was the man for me.

After too few hours of sleep, we were both up and the thrill of the hunt was in the air. David paced the garage, anxious to get started on the sport he'd given up for the mission field. He'd barely slept, but there was no fatigue in his eyes. Like a little boy on Christmas morning, he just wanted the day to dawn. Dave Hale and I both came along on the trip. Being a part of David's world truly excited me; I loved watching the way his eyes lit up at the chance to be back on his home turf.

Once out in the field, the always-dramatic David narrated his movements in a quiet whisper, like a golf tournament: "Only a few hours into the morning, and I get my chance. About 9:00 a.m. we spot two bucks running north across Four States Feedyards' land being chased by a pickup. We try to get in front of them. My pulse races with excitement . . . ." Of course, David's pulse almost always raced with excitement, but this was for a reason he hadn't experienced in many months.

In the end, there was nothing more than the chase. David was mortified that his friend David caught the entire humiliating hunting scene on video (complete with narration and several rounds fired into the field). David was still content and smiling broadly, even without having gotten a good shot. The day finished without a kill, but at least he'd been in the Colorado outdoors, in the hunt (and he did get an antelope the next morning). And the traditional post-hunt cookout at his family's friends, the Stulps, was still ahead.

I'd seen David in Jordan and in Africa and in my hometown, but seeing him in his own "stomping grounds" rounded out my picture of him even more. Meeting his family revealed the source of his values. Going hunting revealed his love of the land and God's creation. The thrill of the hunt revealed another dimension of his passion. He had tried to explain his love for hunting before, but not until experiencing it with him did I understand it. I saw a childlike love and excitement that endeared me to him.

After the cookout we headed back to David's house where I spent time with his mother and sister Sara. We went through old photo albums, and his childhood played out before my eyes. Of course, Sara provided the embarrassing sibling stories, just as my sister Jen had provided for David at my house. It must be a rite of passage into the next phase of a relationship.

David ended the weekend on this romantic note: "I love being with you, Carrie, more than hunting." Before going to Colorado, that statement would have meant something, but after going to Colorado, it meant the world!

CHAPTER THIRTEEN

The Aftermath of 9/11 and a Proposal

The United States—Late Fall 2001

David and I were both in a period of transition. My Journeyman days were over, and I was still thinking about my next assignment. We were both attending seminary and training for our future as career missionaries. Meanwhile, his work in Sudan had become well known in our circles, and with the renewed interest in understanding Islam since 9/11, he was invited to speak on reaching out to Muslims at a church located in the panhandle region.

He put his heart and soul into trying to explain the Muslim world, and how to reach out to them with the gospel. We felt that although politics and war were a necessary evil in the fight against insurgency, only Jesus could be the final answer, and David spoke to that.

A trip to Borger, Texas, allowed him the quiet time he needed to gather his thoughts and seek the Lord. David questioned not only his future in the mission field, but whether I was to be a part of that. He asked God to confirm from the pages of Scripture his wishes that I would be his wife. We were both very cautious with our feelings and actions. We both knew what we wanted: we wanted each other, but we didn't want marriage at the expense of our calling or what the Lord wanted. So we prayed—a lot.

David said these verses gave him the confirmation he was seeking: "Dear children, let us not love with words or tongue but with actions and in truth. This then is how we know that we belong to the truth, and how we set our hearts at rest in his presence whenever our hearts condemn us. For God is greater than our hearts, and he knows everything. Dear friends, if our hearts do not condemn us, we have confidence before God and receive from him anything we ask, because we obey his commands and do what pleases him. And this is his command: to believe in the name of his Son, Jesus Christ, and to love one another as he commanded us" (1 John 3:18–23 NIV).

Although God had given David confidence to move ahead with an engagement to be married, he again expressed his caution to the Lord about not allowing his feelings to make the choice. And again God spoke to his heart: "This then is how we know we belong to the truth, and how we set our hearts at rest in His presence."

David came to realize that an engagement was "treating me with the respect I deserved." Time and time again, David met Christian men who said that when they met their wives-to-be they just knew it was right. He finally understood that if his emotions were grounded in his relationship with the Lord, he should trust them. He finally had the confidence to move towards the next step. I think that with his lifestyle of visiting some of the darkest places on earth and being the first Caucasian in many areas, he had more fears about marriage than a future in Sudan.

He made many attempts, but finally, the words tumbled out of him: "Carrie, I feel like we should get married."

I'd already come to this conclusion and my first thought was,

"What took you so long?" What I actually said was much more diplomatic: "I came to that same conclusion a week ago."

We talked all night until the wee hours of the morning, and David finally left at 5:00 a.m. He was anxious to get married now that the hard part was done (asking me), but I talked him into waiting until June, so I'd have seven months to plan the wedding. We prayed. We talked about rings. And we talked about the verse I'd received to confirm he should be my husband: "For by him all things were created: things in heaven and on earth, visible and invisible, whether thrones or powers or rulers or authorities; all things were created by him and for him. He is before all things, and in him, all things hold together" (Colossians 1:16–17 NIV).

David's parents had met over thirty years earlier on the opening day of pheasant hunting season and held their wedding a year later on opening day. David had come to the same conclusion about his own future on the opening day of pheasant season (November 10, 2001) many years later. He loved the connection of the old and new, and it only confirmed our feelings for one another. We would continue his parents' shared love and the marriage of another generation in love with the Lord.

Of course, once we made the decision we found it completely ridiculous that it had taken as long as it did. How many couples are there who have a passion for the Arab Muslim community and work it out in the field of war and strife? It seems laughable now, but at the time, we were so intent on doing God's will, part of following His will meant not acting in haste.

The official proposal meant a ring and a time frame. We had the date, but we didn't have a ring or formality. David never did anything in his life without flair, and he wanted the proposal to be perfect. So

I waited. I'd like to say I waited patiently, but that wouldn't exactly be true. I was ready for the ring on my finger, a visual reminder to everyone that I would be David McDonnall's wife.

He thought about many different options for how to propose to me. One was a rather public spectacle in a restaurant that included ceremonial *Beja* swords. That one, thank goodness, got nixed. He finally settled on Thanksgiving at my parents' home. That way the family, particularly my mother who already loved him, would come to his rescue if anything went wrong.

Thanksgiving Day 2001 came, and David showed up with three roses, to symbolize the three-corded strand in Ecclesiastes 4:12 (NIV), "Though one may be overpowered, two can defend themselves. A cord of three strands is not quickly broken."

He also had a cookie cake made with the Arabic words *Ana Bahebik* (I love you) in one corner and "Will You Marry Me?" in the center. David told me the lady at the bakery nearly cried when he described it to her.

I said, "Yes!" of course. But David claims he never actually heard the words. He said I only nodded and gave him "good" tears. We were married on June 8, 2002, by our good friend, and David's mentor, Lee.

Our first year of marriage was a blur of activity and careers. We could only afford for one of us to be in seminary, so we decided David would go while he worked three jobs at one time: school bus driver, working the gun counter at a local sporting goods shop, and writing material for a missionary group. I worked as a substitute teacher and at a Lifeway Christian Bookstore. It was a wonderful time of getting to know one another in marriage, but our former lives beckoned.

* * *

As I could have predicted, David and I got restless with seminary. David loved the school bus job, which was a lot of responsibility. He grew attached to his students and took pleasure in shepherding them safely to and from school. But this was a hard time for us because we were used to being in the field. For David to be confined to a classroom to learn about a world he'd already experienced was tedious. We saw seminary as a necessary part of our training and consoled ourselves with the fact that this was temporary. We would be out in the mission field again soon.

For both of us, the call of the Arab world was strong, accentuated by what we saw of the "war on terror" in the media. David and I both felt called to minister to a needy world, and we weren't experiencing that ministry. We often marveled and rejoiced over God's having placed this strong call to serve the Arab world in both our hearts. In fact, I had inscribed his wedding ring with "One Heart," as a reminder of our shared verse, Jeremiah 32:39.

After our first year of marriage, we started an apartment ministry. We worked as a hospitality team, planning activities for those who lived in the apartments, trying to build a community within what is normally a very transitional setting. Both of us loved to entertain and we would host guests in our home as much as possible. David was in his element telling stories about foreign countries while I cooked and often helped set up the stories. It was a wonderful show of our team-work, one we would later use often in Iraq.

We loved being in America and being near our families, but we were homesick for the Arab world. We would sometimes get depressed over not being there, but luckily we kept each other encouraged about our prospects for the future.

During this time of national strife over war and terrorism and boredom for us, David bought me a miniature dachshund we named Macy. I loved that dog, but she quickly turned her allegiance to David. I realize now that she had excellent taste in men.

Still, we missed the Middle East: a place where people took time to stop and smell the roses, to have tea, and just enjoy one another's company. The world moved over there at a different, more social pace. How we missed that sense of hospitality. As we lamented these things, the mission group with whom we had both served in the Middle East told us they were short on teams willing to go into Iraq. Once the fall of Baghdad happened, the U.S. military controlled the borders, and NGOs that had a purpose in the country were welcomed with open arms. With excitement, David and I planned a short-term trip for the summer of 2002 into the once-forbidden country of Iraq.

It was so appropriate that we spent our first anniversary on the mission field in Iraq. David and his longtime team partner, Joseph, led the group. The goal was to nail down logistics like hotels, water sources, and more, so that future teams would be able to come in easily and use the same resources. I saw on this trip how my husband excelled at leadership. He went in with a relatively green team, to a country he'd never visited and came out with an action plan that others could use in the future. He functioned so well in the Arab world, and nowhere was this more evident than in shell-shocked Iraq.

We took in a large team that consisted mostly of women. We quickly moved north, where we worked on a school, refurbishing an auditorium and establishing a computer center. It was a hard mission, as we spent much of the day driving back and forth to the army hospital to fight dehydration. Some of the water we'd purchased turned out to be bad, and so our team, without pure water to drink while they worked under the desert sun, quickly became dehydrated.

In the end, it was a successful trip. I was so overwhelmed by all that God had provided me: a husband who loved me, who loved the same ministry, and who was such an excellent leader. I was in awe of all my life had become.

Ever the romantic, David had a special trip planned in Iraq for our one-year wedding anniversary on June 8, 2003. It not only made me feel special, it showed his ability to maneuver in a country with no infrastructure. He discovered a beautiful stream, and the Iraqi nationals hosting our team baked us a cake. In the hot evening sun, after the long day's work, the water looked inviting and refreshing. Hand in hand, we waded into the water, baptizing ourselves into our first anniversary. We were together, we were doing what we loved, and when the water from that Iraqi river enveloped us, it was as though God Himself touched us and smiled upon us. We were surrounded by others, but in our minds, there were only the two of us under God's heaven.

David, not a singer, began to serenade me with old Garth Brooks songs while Joseph accompanied him on the guitar. He could sing loud, but not well, and the entire group erupted in laughter. I have to say, it ended up more comedic than romantic. But that was truly who David was, and I cherished that moment under the Iraqi sky, having the satisfaction of finishing a humanitarian project, being in a country I never thought I'd see, listening to bad country music sung to me by the man I loved.

After Iraq we continued our anniversary celebration by returning to Eilat, Israel. It was the most appropriate place for us to celebrate our love since it was there that we first began having feelings for one another. We would not have been able to afford such a luxurious getaway in the States. It was our passion to serve the Arabic world that brought us to Eilat the first time and our passion to continue serving that brought us there again. It was a perfect anniversary.

While we were in Israel, a mission supervisor asked us to consider staying on full-time in the Middle East, specifically Iraq. He told us they were in great need of hosts on the ground in Iraq and asked if we would make arrangements to come back and act as hosts and liaisons for future teams and ministries in the country.

"No," David said. "We love this, but we're not going to make a decision here. We have to think about it." David knew that making such a serious decision after our spiritual mountaintop experience in Iraq and Eilat was not a smart choice. It would have been too easy to get caught up in the moment and miss God's long-term direction for our lives.

We put off the decision and went home with the possibility of career mission work in Iraq to consider. Of course, we'd always planned this, and I suppose we always thought we would return to Sudan. When we got back to Texas, without time to decompress, the leadership called us and explained how much they needed us in Iraq. Would we come?

* * *

We were originally asked to come to Iraq permanently by a friend, Jon*. He wanted us to coordinate and spearhead the mission's efforts in northern Iraq. Since David and I both knew the Arabic culture and language, we were a natural fit. Of course, my Arabic was paltry compared to David's fluency, but his management skills were exactly what was needed to coordinate more visiting relief teams in Iraq.

Jon felt we were perfect for the job. With all the displaced peoples, the need for water was huge—and not having to teach us Arabic to get started was a big plus.

We prayed a great deal about it. Iraq was constantly in the news. We knew that life there was not your typical Middle East experience, but we didn't have much time to overanalyze, nor did we really need to. We both felt the desire to go back and discover more about the intriguing world of Daniel's Babylon, Jonah's Nineveh, and Abraham's Ur.

The agency called us on a Thursday and asked if we could give them an answer on Friday, the following day. David and I both went to our respective corners to fast and pray. We didn't want our excitement to get in the way of what God had for us. There was seminary to think about and, although I didn't have much more than a part-time job substitute teaching, we were concerned about dropping our lifestyle on a moment's notice. After praying that night, both of us received the same answer: "Go!"

David received his answer in the gospel of Luke, the passages that talk about leaving all for the sake of the kingdom: "What is impossible with men is possible with God" (Luke 18:27 NIV). "It's one thing," David reflected on this passage, "to hear, profess and believe the truth of that statement while sitting in Sunday school in America, and quite another to be asked to act based on that statement to follow God's calling into a war zone!"

My call came from a different passage, but it was the same message. In the gospel of John, where Jesus fed the five thousand, I heard God telling me to give what little I had and He would bless it abundantly, over and over again (John 6:5–13). Once we said "Yes" to God we were free to say "Yes" to Jon.

David arranged with the seminary to finish out his semester early and get the remainder of his tuition back. We quit our respective jobs and made arrangements to tie up loose ends in Texas.

A mere two months later, we were on our way to Iraq and the adventure of a lifetime. David had such an Indiana Jones lifestyle. He had the hardest time sitting still, and I found that I, having tasted the mission field, couldn't sit still for less myself. I couldn't wait to get started, to get back to the culture I'd missed for nearly two years.

David obviously loved to explore, to encounter new worlds and cultures, but even he was a bit spooked by Iraq. We discovered in the airport in Germany that neither one of us was actually anxious to get to our destination. I was apprehensive because of my past missionary, such as my apartment that turned out to be a portion of a shipping container. I knew things rarely work out as they are expressed in writing or over the telephone. We didn't really know what awaited us, and that resulted in a bit of fear of the unknown. But the truth was, we hadn't said "Yes" to an organization. We had said "Yes" to God. The difference is significant: trusting in man almost always leads to failed expectations. But trusting in God is always safe. We were going to Iraq knowing that God was in control, regardless of what we found when we got there.

David knew that Iraq wasn't safe. The day before we arrived, an RPG-7 (rocket-propelled grenade) had slammed into the oil ministry building and two Baghdad hotels—including the Sheraton Baghdad, where we'd stayed on our last visit. Apparently, this donkey cart-style artillery had the capacity to fire thirty rockets. This was new for us. AK-47s were one thing; RPG-7s were another. The land we were entering had a different set of rules. In addition, we weren't quite sure that our missionary team waiting on the ground was ready.

Before we arrived, two people we'd ministered with during our last visit were literally gunned down in the streets of a northern town. Miraculously, both of them survived. But as you can imagine, the experience tempered our enthusiasm for arrival in a war zone. Although we'd spent lots of time in war-ravaged countries (David had witnessed bomber planes in western Sudan; I'd seen Palestinian suicide bombers and Israeli armor), nothing compared to the all-out warfare going on in Iraq.

David's main prayer requests for our time in Iraq were that God would give us a vision for what He planned to accomplish through us, and that we might establish solid relationships within the Muslim world. Because his main ministries in the Sudan and Eritrea had been so transitory, he hadn't had the opportunity to build the long-term relationships that I had in Israel. After establishing our apartment ministry in Texas and building a community of friends there, we knew that's where both our hearts were.

So he focused on friendships and what we'd do to create them, because they are so very important in the Arab world. As he scribbled into his journal in the German airport, I sighed deeply. I'd never seen David unnerved about entering a country before, and I had my own set of fears. There were lots of questions we didn't have answers to, and they wouldn't be answered until logistics were worked out and we learned our way around. As we looked at one another in the airport, neither of us voiced how truly frightened we were.

As we got ready to board the plane to Jordan, in all honesty, we felt fear, anticipation, skepticism—and to a certain extent, excitement—for the world we were about to experience.

David's fears proved more a reality than my own. When we showed up for duty, our leader, Rich*, had never heard of our team. This was not a good sign, but we saw the situation as if this was the authority God had set before us. And we were there to please God, not a mission leader. Of course, much of our angst was just due to the volatile situation in Iraq, and that couldn't be helped.

For two days, we stayed in Baghdad with other missionaries from an outside team that specialized in construction and rebuilding. The couple we stayed with had long-term experience in Iraq, so we listened intently as they shared their expertise. Their demeanor put us at ease, and we got ready to depart for the north where we'd live.

After traveling by taxi to the northern part of Iraq, about a four- to five-hour trip from Baghdad, we smiled at the site of our new home. The town we'd live in was surrounded by jutting red mountains. Trees, which were rare in Baghdad, lined the streets, and there were paved roads throughout the city. It was in the no-fly zone, protected by the American armed forces, and therefore had an air of safety we coveted.

Our primary concern in Iraq was the large group of IDPs (internally displaced peoples) resulting from human rights abuses committed during Saddam Hussein's reign. In 1999, Hussein called for his countrymen to move north and "Arabize" the Kurdish districts of Kirkuk, Khanaqin, and Sinjar. He called this program "nationality correction" and sought to rid Iraq of its generous Kurd population.

The Kurds are the largest known nationality with no country of their own. They are spread out primarily in Iraq, Turkey, Syria, Iran, Azerbaijan, and Iraq. Although the Kurds are very well organized in Iraq, they have had to fight for their independence constantly—and having their own country seems a far-off dream. But the protection of the American armed forces and their own security forces have kept the Kurdish region in the north relatively free of insurgent attacks and violence.

During their reign, Saddam and the Baathist government sought to control the oil-rich Kurdish parts of the country. Plus, Saddam blamed the Kurds for siding with Iran in the Iran-Iraq war. Saddam claimed the need to stamp out insurgency. In reality, he was single-handedly running an ethnic cleansing campaign. He encouraged Arab southerners, mostly Sunni Muslims, to move north into the Kurdistan area for financial gain. The new laws called for Kurds to identify themselves first and foremost as Arabs or face expulsion from their homes.

At the same time, new Arab settlements were constructed on stolen Kurdish lands, while Kurds were forbidden to sell their homes or other belongings to non-Arabs, making their property worthless. They became nomads, most of them moving north into the wilderness or in with other Kurdish family members. As new census-taking was ordered by Saddam, ethnic cleansing took place until the Kurds were scattered about the outlying areas and into neighboring countries.

This campaign, however, was nothing next to *Anfal*, in which Saddam attacked the Kurds in Halabja in 1988 with chemical weapons, leaving at least 5,000 dead and more than 65,000 with injuries and a legacy of cancer and birth defects. We met a survivor of a family killed by this attack. He'd been a child at the time and had recently found out he had a brother living in a neighboring country who'd been taken out by Kurdish relief workers.

The country has been in turmoil for decades, and as wars and corruption rage, displaced peoples become an unfortunate by-product. When we arrived in the north, many of the displaced Kurds were moving back to their homes in Kurdistan, a non-recognized state within Iraq. Many of the Sunni Arabs who'd moved north under Saddam's guidance were left homeless and in need of shelter. It's a horrible cycle with no easy solution.

Iraq's violent past makes it a country filled with nomads and displaced peoples living in tents or vacated buildings or homes constructed of mud, searching for their next meal, without jobs, and without a functioning government to help them. The list included Kurds from Kirkuk, Khanakin, Mandali, and Mosul. There were also Turkomens, Shiite families, and other minorities. So I knew our job in Iraq, seeing to the needs of these people, many of whom relied on the oil for food program for sustenance, was necessary. We focused on the needs, which were many, heeding our call for Arab Muslims near the Mosul area. We didn't focus on our lack of a solid plan. Plans get changed in these countries anyway, so we simply went to work.

Once we were stationed in our northern city with another mission team, there was a constant flow of volunteer teams needing our hospitality, and several immediate distribution projects. We assisted in distributing two shipping containers full of food and 9,000 blankets. Needless to say, we weren't exactly "nesting," and still hadn't found a permanent home in the neighborhood.

Add to this the fact that distribution projects were a call to trouble. Not only did moving a load of survival kits make you a soft target, but they could be seen as political favors, rife with corruption and the potential to turn into instant chaos. One such project, with another team, went terribly wrong in Baghdad and a mob of people literally broke out windows and doors in an effort to get to the food that was to be distributed. Fortunately, our distribution projects suffered no such violent ends.

During this time, we had to drive to Mosul to repair a pick-up truck that had been shot full of holes when the last team had been attacked. That vehicle was going to be ours, and it did nothing to calm our nerves. We were uncomfortable driving a vehicle that had already been targeted during an attack, but if we repaired and painted it, the truck would appear like any of a thousand such trucks in northern Iraq. We took solace in that fact and made arrangements for the repairs.

After this first round of projects that lasted a few weeks, we went back to Amman, Jordan, for a short respite before settling permanently in Iraq. Jordan felt so westernized. We arrived during the last two days of Ramadan, but we did get to enjoy one of David's favorite parts of the Muslim holy days: the Pizza Hut Ramadan buffet, where you get all-you-can-eat pizza after dark.

We were still newlyweds, and after our fabulous dinner, we had coffee at the Amman Hilton and saw a movie, *Pirates of the Caribbean*. It was like being in America for a time, but with the Arab culture we loved surrounding us—sort of a "best of both worlds" scenario.

The next day in Jordan was filled with meetings, and one of them was our first contact with Karen Watson, who would be with us on our fateful day in Mosul. Karen was thirty-eight years old, from Bakersfield, California. She'd lived in Baghdad before the pressures of Iraq caused her to take a brief retreat from the country and move back home. Now she was considering another move into Iraq, and we talked about those possibilities.

After meeting with Karen, we met with Jared*, an Arab and fellow believer. He had always been open to the Word, but had never made a commitment to Christ, until he had been injured in an attack in northern Iraq. Now, as he spoke to us through jaws wired shut, Jared told us he'd become a believer in Jesus as a result of the attack on his life. Jesus had saved him that terrible day, he said. "My Jesus is in my blood."

David's face lit up. I'll never forget the encouragement Jared's testimony of faith brought to him. David was upset the attack had happened, yet he rejoiced with the heavens that the walk had been completed for Jared. You couldn't wash the smile from David's face the rest of the day. He knew that God was sovereign, and that even in awful circumstances, God was at work.

Our excitement continued as we returned to Iraq, where we learned that Saddam Hussein had been captured hiding in the bottom of a hole.

CHAPTER FOURTEEN

Saddam Hussein's Capture

Baghdad, Iraq—December 14, 2003

After our whirlwind tour in Jordan, we drove back to Baghdad to meet with other team members before finishing the long drive back to our home in the north. It turned out to be quite an interesting day in Baghdad—the day American forces captured Saddam Hussein.

"Living in Iraq is tough, but on this day there's no place I'd rather be," David wrote in his journal of Saddam's capture.

At 8:30 p.m. local time, Coalition forces captured Saddam Hussein south of his hometown of Tikrit (halfway between Baghdad and the northern area). Jubilant crowds filled the streets of Iraq. Turkmen, Kurds, Arabs, Shia, and Sunni all joined together in the celebration. After decades of fractures and factions, and the constant battle for power, all fighting stopped as the Iraqi people rejoiced at the prospect of Saddam's finally being brought to justice. Naturally, it wouldn't take long for fighting to start back up again, but for this one day, there was widespread peace. We were very much aware that we were living in the middle of history's being made.

Even before Coalition authorities made the official announcement, there was dancing in the streets, AK-47s being fired into the
air, cars parading through the streets honking their horns, drivers
and riders throwing candy to the crowds. Finally, at 2:30 p.m.,
Baghdad grew quiet as everyone, including us, gathered around tele-
visions to hear Paul Bremer, U.S. Civilian Administrator in Iraq,
make the announcement: "Ladies and gentlemen . . . we got him!" At
Bremer's words, the military and civilian audience to whom he was
speaking directly erupted in cheers. And there was cheering all over
Baghdad and the rest of Iraq as well.

Some of the Iraqi press shouted, "Death to Saddam!" in Arabic.
Finally, Bremer turned the news conference over to General Ricardo
Sanchez, U.S. Forces Commander, who gave details of the capture.
When videotape of Saddam's receiving a medical exam was shown,
revealing a bedraggled and impotent former leader, cheers and
shouts erupted again.

The Arab media stood again and chanted, "Death to Saddam!
Death to Saddam!"

This emotion reached all levels of society. Our Iraqi driver, who
we used while in Baghdad, came into our room. Seeing Saddam on
television, he clapped and said, "They found him hiding like a rat.
Like a rat in a hole!" (In contrast, the streets of Tikrit, Saddam's
hometown and the center of his Baathist party, were said to be
deathly quiet when the news broke.)

We watched the coverage with several Iraqis in our room. They
were glued to the television. A mixture of excitement and disbelief
was on their faces, until they saw the video of Saddam's medical
exam. Then their expressions visibly changed—their faces flooded
with relief as if it was okay to believe that the tyrant who had ruined
their lives was finally in custody. It was if a curtain was pulled back

that had been obscuring the future of the country until Saddam was caught. Of course, the road to the future was not immediately paved with ease and convenience and still is not today. But with the capture of Saddam came the first tangible evidence that hope was a possibility.

Tears and heartfelt thanks welled up inside me as I witnessed such raw emotion and hope on the part of our Iraqi friends. To play a small part in the lives of such a resilient people was truly a gift from the Lord.

Every detail of Saddam's capture was devoured by the people of Iraq. U.S. troops learned on December 13, 2003, that Saddam was likely in one of two locations in a village south of Tikrit. Nearly 600 troops began "Operation Red Dawn" at about 6:15 p.m. Saddam was found in one of the locations, hiding in an underground bunker—literally, a small, man-sized hole dug in the ground with a camouflaged cover over the top. No bodyguards, no army, no limousines, no gold-plated fixtures. Just a dirt hole—a "spider hole," as the military and media termed it. It was an ignominious end for a dictator with a $25 million bounty on his head. Suddenly the Iraqi people saw Saddam for who he was. He had a pistol with him, but he chose not to fight against his enemy. He just gave up, apparently unwilling to risk the same end to which he had sentenced thousands of his own subjects: death. The Iraqis laughed at him and his cowardly demise.

The celebration was short-lived, of course, as the reality of a war zone quickly set in. The day we drove in from Jordan we saw two U.S. Blackhawk helicopters set down in the distance ahead of us. As we approached the scene, we saw that a U.S. military convoy had stopped on the westbound side of the highway. Soldiers stood at the ready with their weapons while armed and armored Humvees blocked the road. There were two stretchers on the pavement—we knew there had been a roadside ambush. We never found out the details of the attack on that convoy—Saddam's capture overshadowed everything else the next several days. It was a simple reminder that we were heading into a war zone. And while we were not going to be stationed in Baghdad, it did not take long for us to realize that the Iraqi insurgency was going to continue to wreak havoc all over Iraq, even in the north. For some reason, seeing the attacked convoy and the wounded soldiers that day did not make us want to leave. It only heightened our resolve to work hard and learn how to take care of ourselves and the people we were there to help.

The difficulties were left behind, as throughout the day gunfire and horns continued in celebration. Even during our team's weekly prayer meeting, AK-47 gunfire exploded through the air. David, trying to lighten the atmosphere, teased, "You might be in Iraq if you've ever had a prayer meeting interrupted by gunfire."

On our way home to our guesthouse from the prayer meeting, we asked a neighbor's guard if we could pop off a few rounds on the AK-47. Somehow it just seemed like a necessary part of the celebration.

The guard consented and chambered a round, clipped off the safety and held the rifle to the air. David was surprised at how slight the recoil was—nearly nothing. Perhaps this wasn't one of our more shining moments in Iraq, but it was quite an adventure, and David, being ever the adventurer, couldn't resist. Firing an AK-47 in Baghdad to celebrate Saddam's capture made for quite a day.

When we got to our home in the north, we praised God for that day. It was a monumental day in history and we had been there to watch it happen, to appreciate the capture's full effects on the Arab people. Just one day before or after, we would have not been in

Baghdad, so we were grateful for God's sovereign timing. There was so much pain and suffering in Iraq that it was wonderful to see the people rejoice and be full of hope for a day. Seeing their joy and their hope that something might change brought us hope and determination.

There were differing opinions though. Another Iraqi taxi driver told us, "I won't fully believe it until I see Saddam myself." We asked him if he wished for Saddam's death as the media had chanted the day before, and he replied, "I think Saddam should be kept in an open prison where everyone in Iraq could go and see him behind bars. They would be able to yell at him and hit him if they liked."

When we passed through the Kurdish area, the Kurds were over-joyed at the capture. Several made it clear the only choice was to execute the man immediately. (Remember: thousands of the Kurds had been killed by Saddam's chemical warfare/ethnic cleansing strategy. They were relieved he no longer had the power to harm them.) So although Saddam's capture brought excitement throughout Iraq, what to do with him was met with varying ideas, most involving some level of violence.

As we bumped along the road to our northern town, we realized how familiar we'd become with this stretch of highway in yet another orange and white taxi cab. Sometimes the road was muddy, some-times slick with rain, but we could always count on it to be bumpy and rough and driven at breakneck speeds by cab drivers anxious to get off the endless sand dunes and into civilization. To think of Texas where people would go "four-wheeling" for pleasure became a bit of a joke. It said a lot about Saddam's regime that the two major cities in the country (Mosul and Baghdad) were not connected by a well-kept highway, though Saddam had many palaces in the city of Baghdad alone. The country had no infrastructure, no safety net for its people, and no economy to speak of that benefitted anyone but Saddam and his Baathist party.

Our brief visit to Amman, Jordan, to meet with the team leader had resulted in more questions than answers. As we headed north on the makeshift road, we had no idea what we were stepping into with this new, undefined ministry. We learned on that trip we'd be addressing the needs of the Arab-Muslim population in the north of Iraq, primarily the needs of Mosul and the area west of the city. One of our concerns was that we wouldn't be setting up our homestead in this area. Rather, we'd be housed in a safer area that had more of a U.S. military presence. Given our past experience working with Arab Muslims, we felt that working with them during the day, then running for cover at night, would not give us the credibility with them we knew it would take to build serious relationships. Without defined relationships and friendships with the Arab Muslims, we worried that our presence would never be fully accepted.

Of course, our mission organization had good reason to place us where they did. Mosul was growing increasingly difficult with more riots and attacks, and it was even considered dangerous for armed soldiers. Just a few days before we arrived, there had been a large riot in Mosul and an American convoy was attacked on the road between Irbil and Mosul, a road we'd traveled often. Apparently, hearing the word "Mosul" on American television started a frantic phone-calling session by our families and the mission board until they heard we were safe and sound.

So with a harsh reality check, we realized living in Mosul was not a possibility. But in the Arab world where relationships were key, this was a source of contention for us. In addition to not living where we'd planned, we were living in the Kurdish area where Arabic was not even spoken. So we felt out of our element and out of God's will. Our mission was in Mosul, and we weren't there.

Despite this situation, we signed a year's lease on a two-story furnished home in a Kurdish area of Iraq—the closest, safest territory near Mosul. The walls of the house were of white tile with gold designs; the furnishings were also gold and white. And the stairs were made of marble and stone. It was a nice home in spite of the trek to the rooftop for the generator (at least we had a generator). Electricity in Iraq is spotty, and often a maximum of four hours a day of electricity is all you get. Only people with generators have electricity around the clock.

The neighborhoods in northern Iraq are quite nice, with two- and three-story homes built of concrete. They don't differ that much from American neighborhoods except for the absence of lawns and trees. In wealthier neighborhoods the houses are more architecturally diverse—with turrets and the like. The chief difference between houses in the Kurdish neighborhoods and those back home, was that many houses came complete with a guard station, where private security guards would stand day and night.

Although I'd gotten used to the pungent odor of kerosene lanterns for light, using the generator for electric lights was much preferred. A generator was a sign of wealth where we lived, so we kept it well-protected and concealed on the roof. Our oven was a gas-fired contraption that required lighting the pilot each time it was used. I tried it once and it belched smoke and fumes into the kitchen that took a day to dissipate. So I avoided the oven like the plague but used the stovetop and a nice toaster oven to cook our meals.

Shopping in Iraq meant going to various stores at the market-place for different items instead of one central supermarket. The shops are very small, most being no bigger than ten feet square, and most are outfitted with a pull-down, locking garage-type door that covers the front of the shop when it is closed. Shelves were stocked with various canned or boxed food, and only boxed milk was available. Eggs, frozen chicken, and candy were a few of the staples most stores stocked. You could purchase laundry detergent and cleaning products, even toilet paper, though that was the only paper product they carried. Paper napkins and paper towels were a luxury we did without.

Fresh vegetables could be purchased at the vegetable stand, and we had access to tomatoes, lettuce, green onions (the size of golf balls and hot!), garlic, zucchini, bell pepper, cucumbers, and more. Although most of the fresh foods were imported from surrounding countries, they were never in short supply, even as the war raged on.

The meat shops were one of the biggest differences from life in the States. Meats of all kinds hung from the door's frame and the rafters. They stocked goat and lamb and sometimes beef (the most expensive). All of the carcasses were dressed with the animals' heads lying on the ground, innards to the side. You'd tell the store owner what you wanted and how much, and he'd slice that amount off the carcass, weigh it, and put it in a small bag. The shops usually had meat grinders in the back, but I preferred to grind my own meat since the butchers wouldn't strip the membrane off the meat before grinding it. The membrane was left on the meat while it hung in the open air as a barrier against the flies. Fish from the local rivers was also available, but that seemed a bit riskier to me, so I was especially careful when choosing fish. Additionally, I would use filtered water and a special vegetable wash for the fresh produce. I'm proud to say that we never got sick from food I prepared, in spite of eating lots of meat that had hung in the hot sun and eating vegetables of unknown origin.

The one thing we missed immensely was our beloved Dr. Pepper, which could be bought in the Green Zone in Baghdad (a large protected enclave in Baghdad providing goods and services to soldiers and civilians that were not available in Baghdad generally), but not where we were settled. Soda was available, particularly Pepsi, but it came in tall, slender cans and had about half the serving of a can at home.

Our presence in the north was not necessarily something that the local Iraqi people noticed. Iraqi men would approach David if they heard him speaking Arabic, and I would be approached on occasion by beggar women. It was mostly children who approached us freely. They would come up to us and stare, try to speak with us, or simply walk alongside of us. Even if they spoke Kurdish, rather than Arabic, our smiles were a universal language. David and I loved to host parties and invite people into our home, and as soon as we became adept at cooking on the new stovetop, we began to make our home the center of the social activity we loved. Our home was very comfortable and we were soon hosting many visiting mission teams, as well as getting to know our neighbors.

While we still were not completely in step with the oversight and support being provided for our ministry, we were comforted by a passage of Scripture David read—the story of Saul's blinding conversion on the road to Damascus (Acts 9:10–16 NIV). In Damascus, God spoke to Ananias and told him to go and lay hands on Saul so he would receive his sight. Ananias knew of the infamous Saul's reputation as a killer of Christians and offered a mild objection: "'Lord,' Ananias answered, 'I have heard many reports about this man and all the harm he has done to your saints in Jerusalem. And he has come here with authority from the chief priests to arrest all who call on your name.' But the Lord said to Ananias, 'Go! This man is my chosen instrument to carry my name before the Gentiles and their kings and before the people of Israel. I will show him how much he must suffer for my name.'"

This passage comforted David at this time in our uprooted lives. From a Christian's perspective, Saul was the last person the church would choose to spread the gospel, especially to the Gentiles, since Saul was such an educated Jew. But God sees what we don't, and Ananias had to obey God's directive even though he didn't understand it. Sometimes, God's ways don't make sense, and at this point in our ministry, they didn't make sense to us either. As a result of Ananias' obedience in a seemingly dangerous situation, Saul (Paul) became the greatest missionary in all of church history. We clung to that as we waited for word to go into Mosul on a permanent basis.

We prayed to be faithful to what God called us to, and leave the timing and results up to Him. We went about our daily routine, keeping the house ready for visiting teams, meeting with neighbors, and making new friends. The language barrier was an issue, but most of the Kurds spoke some Arabic, so we worked from that base. The peoples' warm smiles and Texas-type hospitality made us feel right at home, and we relished the affection we received from the Kurdistan people. Our home was run like an open house, and we often had neighbors or friends in for Arab coffee and hot tea.

I dare anyone to look into the deep brown or brilliant blue eyes of an Iraqi child and not want to help. The Kurds were independent in many ways, and many of them were Catholics who knew Christ. It was the Sunni Muslims whom we hoped to reach for the Lord and help lift from their darkness.

War was with us always during our time there. Machine gun fire became standard fare, and only when a big explosion sounded did we look at each other questioningly. The low-flying helicopters and sight of AK-47s were constant.

Once we were settled, we made the long, arduous trip back to Amman, Jordan, to meet with our supervisors. After those meetings we were hustled back to Baghdad.

CHAPTER FIFTEEN

Christmas in Baghdad

Baghdad, Iraq—Christmas 2003

The Christmas season was hard for both of us. We'd been in Iraq for little more than a month, and we were thousands of miles from home, celebrating the birth of our Savior in an unfamiliar place with kind, but mostly unfamiliar and non-Christian people. We missed our family, we missed America, and we felt a little lost in the wilderness of explosive Baghdad. Our ministry had yet to come to full fruition, and at Christmas we felt the uncertainty of a lack of true purpose in a war-torn nation.

We wanted to be in Mosul making a difference with the Arab Muslims we felt called to assist. The very thought of living outside the Arab area truly discouraged David. He thrived on learning more Arabic and befriending those of the Arab culture; he came alive when he got to speak the language with Arabs. We both loved the relationships and customs of the people, yet within our neighborhood, he didn't speak the language and we were still learning their different customs. Yes, we were making inroads, but in a

Christian part of Iraq. It felt as though we were in a holding pattern, missing our true purpose of why we were called to the country in the first place.

Even the gift-giving season was somewhat marred by practicality. A few weeks before Christmas, David began asking me, "Do you want to get a meat grinder?"

It was a practical thing. A meat grinder would allow us to prepare our own meat and ensure its safety. But I thought David was getting overenthusiastic in telling me how much I would enjoy my very own meat grinder. Knowing the logistics of the Iraqi marketplace, I knew that my choices were limited in that there was only so much to purchase. To buy David's gift, I would need him with me, as it wasn't proper for a woman to be alone in the market. So the Christmas season was destined to be different.

"Don't you really want a meat grinder?" David would ask.

And I thought, *He's really going to get me a meat grinder for Christmas.* Finally I said to him while at the marketplace, "You're not really going to get me a meat grinder for Christmas are you? You know about the rule, right?"

"What rule?" David asked.

"About not buying your wife appliances for Christmas."

"Oh," David said, his expression downcast. "No, I didn't know about the rule." He paused a moment. "What if I took it back before the holidays?"

"No." I said, "If you bought me an appliance for Christmas, you have to own up to it. You can make up for it next Christmas."

I knew by his shocked expression that he had indeed bought me a meat grinder, thinking I would enjoy it. I was surprised, but in a lighthearted, this-is-Christmas-in-Iraq sort of way. As we exited the marketplace, I saw that he'd had the box all wrapped up in his jacket, and his eyes just smiled when he knew he'd been caught. It was the newlywed's lament: an appliance on Christmas.

A few days later, he took me down to the gold market and bought me some tiny gold heart earrings and a heart pendant. I knew those things were coming on Christmas, but I was still looking forward to seeing the meat grinder, his true idea of a present. By the time Christmas Eve rolled around, I actually couldn't wait to see it.

He'd joked about it for some time, about how it was the perfect gift and how he'd be the champion of a husband to get it for me. When I finally unwrapped the package and saw a meat grinder box, I laughed uproariously.

"Open it," David said.

"I know what a meat grinder looks like, David."

"Go ahead; open it."

So I did, and inside was a typical black marketplace bag. "You just got me the box!"

I pulled out the bag and inside was a beautiful snow globe I had admired back in Texas. Just before we left for Iraq, David had surprised me with a trip to my beloved alma mater, Texas A&M. When we were in the mall, and he saw me looking at the Aggie globe, he knew by my face that I wanted it. But after one look at the price, I knew it was something for collectors only.

Once we left that store, David had pretended to go to the bathroom and left me standing in the mall. Apparently, he'd gone back to the store, purchased the snow globe, snuck it out to the car, and come back for me. I'd started to worry he'd gotten lost. He had snuck the snow globe into our apartment, hid it while we packed up the apartment to move our belongings into storage, and then kept it hidden countless times as we packed and unpacked for Iraq. Not only had he planned ahead, he got me the most precious gift I could have imagined—something he knew would truly make me happy.

I'm an Aggie through and through, so having that treasure from home meant the world to me; it made the day feel a bit more like the Christmas holiday I knew. In return, I had gone to great lengths to keep hidden the Christmas gift I brought from the States for David— a hunting video game for his X-Box game player.

Our gift exchange was the highlight of Christmas Eve day, but after an anticlimactic Christmas Eve, David and I turned in early. We slept through the distant but persistent and unmistakable sounds of war; bombs, explosions, and the familiar *buzz* of Gatling guns rattled our nerves, but not our sleep—until war came too close.

Christmas morning in Baghdad began at 6:15 when we were jolted from bed by the sound of a close explosion, followed by the distinct whistle of an incoming mortar or rocket. We looked at one another, hoping against hope that the whistle wouldn't end in our guesthouse. With relief we heard the rocket whish right by us and land somewhere else with a thud. Time stood still as we listened to hear whether another whistle would break the silence.

It was an unusually violent day in Iraq, with bombs and explosions throughout the day: sirens wailing, windows rattling, planes screaming, helicopters chopping. It was impossible to make sense of any of the noises, to know who was bombing whom. It was just constant chaos. Christmas in Iraq was fraught with violence that year, and it did little to lighten our moods.

Iraq is three percent Christian, and normally Baghdad would have been quite festive on Christmas day. But this year was solemn with the war in the background. No one wanted to attract too much attention for fear of not knowing who would be in power. And let's face it, the sound of bombs doesn't exactly put one in the Christmas spirit. So the absence of all the decorations and festivities around town only served as a reminder that this was Christmas in a war zone. I can only imagine how all the American servicemen and women felt, being away from their families on Christmas morning.

Later that Christmas morning with the rest of our team, rather than discuss how completely unnerved we were by the close call, we argued whether it was a mortar round or a rocket. David was convinced it was a mortar round and discussed it as an aficionado of modern weaponry the way other people around the Christmas table might discuss the fruitiness of the wine.

After our morning discussion of artillery sounds, we assembled around a large table in the guesthouse and sat down for a traditional Iraqi breakfast: crisp bread topped with cheese and honey. Very fattening, but very much worth the calories.

After our meal, we held our gift exchange. Because we had participated in drawing names by e-mail before we arrived in Baghdad, somehow there was a mix-up and no one had a gift for David. It was a small thing but contributed to making our first Christmas in Iraq a "downer" for us. We really had nothing to do, and rather than wallow in our feelings, we each took a nap.

Christmas 2003 stripped us of all the peripherals of the holiday, things that we take for granted in the States: family, gifts, trees, parties, and friends. We focused on the One Who brought us to Iraq, and the knowledge that His call was trustworthy.

After a quick trip to Jordan to pick up a new team, we arrived back in Baghdad and stayed with a permanent missionary family who'd been stationed for eight years in Indonesia. The Smith's* extensive experience working with Muslims had resulted in numerous conversions to Christ. They were a solid couple who seemed to bear great fruit for the Lord. Meeting them made us long even more for the time we would plant our roots in Mosul and see fruit of our own.

CHAPTER SIXTEEN

On the Bumpy Road Back—
Happy New Year!

Northern Iraq and Baghdad—January 2004

David and I returned to our home in the Kurdish area with the team. David had been going through the house, filling the heaters and lamps with kerosene while a friend and I chatted and made hot tea in the kitchen. Suddenly David walked into the kitchen with something tucked under his arm.

He shouted, "Happy New Year, baby! Here's a New Year's gift for you." And he put the meat grinder onto the counter! We all laughed uproariously as he declared, "See, it's not a Christmas gift, so it's okay!" The man was full of surprises. Even in discouraging times, he could do something in some memorable way that produced a beautiful result.

We had returned with two new volunteers who were fresh and enthusiastic about their assignment. They were two young women we had known from seminary in Texas, and their enthusiasm was motivational for us. We were thrilled to have them! We'd known they were coming for some time, so we had time to prepare and make appropriate arrangements for them.

I finally felt worthy of my hostess role and was excited to have women around me. They became great friends, prayer partners, and soul mates. It was wonderful to have women friends in whom to confide emotionally. Talking openly with them kept me from having to burden David, knowing he had his own level of despair about not being able to move into Mosul.

A second team of four women and two men arrived. Combined with the first team, we now had a strong group of volunteers, but little to do for so many eager hands. We began work on the Widow's Project with the two teams of women in our living room. The Widow's Project was a place where young women in Iraq were given education and taught a trade for themselves. We worked on teaching crafts and the finer arts that would still be considered feminine in their world.

In this particular case, our visiting team of women taught the ladies how to create greeting cards with stamps. It was such an American project, such a docile activity in the midst of full-scale war that waged outside the Kurdish region. But stamping truly had universal appeal, and we sounded like any other group of ladies gathered for a social day, though none of us could communicate with one another.

The widows spoke Kurdish, I spoke English and Arabic, and a local team member spoke Spanish and Kurdish. The two visiting seminary students spoke Spanish and English. Thus, by providing those two young women, God had given us a way to communicate with the Kurdish widows. I would translate in Arabic to our assistant, and she would translate to one of the Spanish speakers in Kurdish, and then she'd repeat in Spanish. Together, we laughed and made crafts and felt like we were being effective with the women in the region.

When David came home that day, the house was a mess with scraps of paper and supplies all over the floor. But he was excited to see the evidence of so much productive activity. Of course, I was anxious because the house was a sty! (A messy house is a reflection upon the man in Arab cultures, not the woman—and I was still without a vacuum cleaner.) Naturally, a male neighbor picked that time to stop by for a visit, and I was totally embarrassed by the appearance of the house. The man's face fell as he saw the condition of our home. Of course, nothing was mentioned. That would have been considered rude.

We got through the transitional time and sent the last temporary teams home, feeling like we could finally focus on the ministry God had brought us to Iraq to accomplish. We were ready to work on water distribution for the displaced Arabs living in the vicinity. We also felt like we were finally getting support from our team leader and would be able to trade out the vehicle with all the bullet holes in it. Something about that truck never set right with David, and though not a suspicious or fearful man, he was thankful for a newer, quality vehicle. We praised God for our good fortune.

Finally, we received permission to begin looking for a home in Mosul, where the Sunni Arabs to whom we felt called were located. We were told we could go as soon as we were ready. David and I literally jumped for joy at this news. We had felt like airplanes circling the field for months, and now we were being given permission to land. *Just get out of our way*, we thought. We also learned we'd be getting a new team leader, and we prayed for better communication this time. It was a chance to start fresh, to make another leader understand our vision and love for the Sunni Arabs.

Our new team leader had Middle East experience and had been in Jordan, the home of David's original ministry. We took that as a positive sign and happily went to Baghdad to finalize the arrangements. This time, we had the privilege of entering the famous Green Zone.

The Green Zone is a little slice of America smack-dab in the center of Baghdad. The area is actually comprised of many of Saddam's former palaces and former government buildings and takes up several square miles of space. After a lengthy security check through many gates and barricades, we visited the US-AID offices, which were housed in a modern convention center—especially nice for Iraq, considering the state of the rest of the country.

It was impossible not to long for home at the sight of what was available for sale in the Green Zone. In a store something like a mini-Wal-Mart, there were a variety of foods, electronics, books—everything we could have gotten back in the U.S. Yet it was no bigger than a gas-convenience store. We splurged on Chips Ahoy cookies and DVDs from the army store that was across the street from Saddam's former palace.

It was amazing to think that the palaces from which Saddam had run roughshod over his country a year before were now filled with American military personnel. The Green Zone was an interesting oasis in the midst of a desert of war. As soon as we were finished with our shopping and meetings, we were thankful to return to the relative quiet of northern Iraq.

We first spoke about the move to Mosul with a good friend and longtime resident of the Kurdish area. He was concerned about our plans, warning us of all the attacks that the various groups in Mosul were known for carrying out against one another and against anyone connected with the Coalition that had taken over Iraq—which included Americans like us. The "Muslim Brotherhood" or *Hamas*, and the even more deadly *Wahhabis*, were very active in

Mosul at the time. Our desire to move into town was tempered by this latest information about how bad the current conditions were in the city. The residents of the city we longed to move into were a virtual who's who of terrorist organizations, and this stopped us in our tracks. More information would have to be gathered before we left the relative safety of the Kurdish area. We knew what we were getting ourselves into, but David's journal entries were almost prophetic, showing his heart. He was willing to give all for Christ.

At the time, David wrote, "Yes, it's dangerous. Yes, we could die, but Paul faced the exact same dangers, and he faced them boldly, keeping his eyes on finishing his race with joy and being obedient to his call to share the Gospel. This kind of boldness is exactly what I need. Lord, give me the boldness to carry Your name to those who may wish to do me harm. Give me wisdom, but more than that, give me courage, strength and boldness to simply be obedient to hear your call."

To further assess our planned move, we met with Coalition forces in Mosul to discuss the humanitarian needs we saw and wanted to address. The forces were housed in one of Saddam's marble palaces. On the stairway, there was a marble mosaic of Saddam holding a little girl in his lap. The little girl looks terrified in the arms of the dictator, yet the scene is supposed to give the impression that this is a man who loved his people. The little girl's eyes seem to reach out to passersby begging for help to escape his clutches. I wondered why they would create a mosaic with such a terrified look on the girl's face.

There was another mosaic of an Arab woman in traditional covering. The whole interior was meant to be warm, to reflect the people of Iraq. Yet it felt like the most evil place, like being in a cold, dead tomb—the haunting eyes of the Arab woman staring at you, the little girl who looked so frightened you want to rip her out of the mosaic. After seeing these images, which is as close as I'd ever want to come to Saddam Hussein, we discussed security risks and the reality of moving into Mosul.

As we listened to the Coalition representatives explain the risks, our ministry was at a crossroad. Were we not listening to God clearly? Did we belong in the Kurdish area instead of Mosul? Or did God truly want us to reach out in faith and trust Him with the risks? Why did we have such a heart for reaching Muslim Arabs if we were being warned about how dangerous it might be?

We kept studying the life of the apostle Paul and reading about his entrance into Rome, the most important center of government in the world at the time. It was not a place that was sympathetic to the gospel of the lordship of Christ, and his path into that place had not been easy. He'd been in prison, shipwrecked on the way to Rome, bitten by a deadly snake, and delivered from death. And finally he got to Rome because it was God's will. As we waited, we believed if God wanted us in Mosul, He would prepare the way just as He did for Paul to get to Rome.

God gave us His answer, but not in the way we expected. We never got to Mosul. The insurgent ambush happened before we had a chance to conclude whether the move was safe or not. I think about our little house in the Kurdish area and our life together there, and I'm so grateful for that time now. After the attack, David was airlifted to Baghdad. I was airlifted to Kuwait, then to Landstuhl, Germany, and after eight days of a drug-induced coma, I finally woke up in a Dallas, Texas, hospital.

CHAPTER SEVENTEEN

After the Attack

Dallas, Texas—March 2004

That evening in Iraq, while David and I were being operated on in the sixty-seventh CSH (Combat Support Hospital) unit, our good friend Lee called my mother to tell her the news of our attack. Lee was like family, and my mother never expected his phone call to lead to anything more than a friendly conversation.

My mother, a hospital operating room director and R.N., was at her desk as usual on a Monday morning around ten. After seeing that all the surgeries for the day were on schedule, she was checking e-mail. The phone call wasn't out of the ordinary and my mother was thrilled to hear from Lee.

"This is Margaret," she said in her strong southern accent. "Lee! What are you doing calling me?"

He didn't pause. He blurted it out to get it over with. "David and Carrie have been shot. They were shot in Mosul." Lee went on to say that I had been rushed into surgery, and that David had called his boss, Jon, on the satellite phone to tell him of the attack. Lee explained we were both alive, and that we'd been with the Elliotts and Karen Watson, who had all died in the attack. David and I were still alive. There were no further details, and I don't think my mom needed any. She was in complete shock.

My mom sank to the floor and crumpled beneath her desk, her heart pounding and her breathing short. As she did so, a friend saw her from the doorway and rushed to her side. She knew instinctively it was about me in Iraq. What else would send my mother, who is normally calm, into such a state? While Lee kept talking into the phone, my mother tried to decipher what she'd heard and to pray with the co-worker who'd come to her aid. The friend began to pray over her and for David and me.

This was the beginning of the targeting of NGOs in Iraq. Within the next two days, more grim news came about American civilians who were killed, burned and hung from a bridge in Falluja. But for now, the idea of "soft targets" was not yet a household word associated with Iraq. Fortunately, my mother didn't know how ugly things could get. That was a saving grace for her as she tried to comprehend that her daughter might not be coming home.

Only the day before, a Sunday in Iraq, my mom had talked to David on the Elliotts' cell phone. She told me then that it seemed she always talked to me and she missed the sound of David's voice. The two of them talked for a while, and David entertained her with stories as he always did. They used to get into deep theological discussions. They had a mutual fan club, my mother and David. For his birthday, just twenty short days before, she'd sent him the following e-mail:

I miss...
   Your big, booming voice that fills the room with joy and brings a smile to my face.

Your laughter that travels right up to your eyes and tells everyone that you are sincere and honest.

The way you look at my daughter with a love that will last a lifetime.

The way you shamelessly kiss up to your mother-in-law.

Your pocket knife, when no one else around me has one.

Your love of the outdoors, camping, campfires; we would be planning a spring break trip even now.

Going to church with you, and seeing how you love to praise and worship Him.

The way you always play with my grandchildren.

Your stories, your stories, your stories.

Your abiding and calm spirit at times of stress.

Your great big, bear hugs, knowing you really mean it.

Our discussions about the Word.

YOU, and the way you remind me of HIM.

We all love you and are so proud of who you are. In His Mighty Hands I leave you.

Love always,
Margaret Taylor

I don't imagine there are many mothers-in-law who send their son's-in-law fan letters like that. I think it speaks to David's warmth and how people were just drawn to him. My mother trusted David. She knew he wouldn't foolishly go into danger himself or lead me into danger unnecessarily. And, in fact, that's why he had held back from Mosul for so long.

When my mother recovered enough to think about the phone call she'd just received, she thought instantly of my father. She called my sister immediately and asked Jen to meet her at home. My dad was working nights then and my mom wanted to make sure he didn't get a call from our mission supervisor, or the media, before she'd had a chance to tell him. Mom and my sister Jennifer rushed home and, fortunately, beat my father home.

By the time Mom got home, clips of David entering the Iraqi hospital were all over CNN. My nephew was saying, "Look Mama, there's Uncle David on the TV."

In the video, David looked fine. He was alert and talking, propped up with his hands locked behind his head, giving the distinct message, "I'm okay." So at home they prepared for the news of *my* death, not David's. David was fine, they reasoned, they'd seen him talking on television.

As a nurse, my mother was aware that being rushed into surgery was never a good thing, so in everyone's mind back home in Texas, I was the most critical. I'd been hit twenty-two times by bullets and shrapnel. In the CSH unit outside Mosul they had immediately pumped me full of blood that wasn't screened for antibodies, which is only done when a patient is so near death there isn't time for screening. They gave me numerous strong antibiotics and left all my wounds open rather than closing in the bacteria. Apparently the bullets used by insurgents in Iraq are stored in such unsanitary conditions that they come loaded with bacteria and germs. Besides the physical damage they cause, they are like airborne contamination delivery systems.

Back at home, my mother informed my father of my condition and frantically worked to get to Landstuhl Regional Medical Center in Germany where I was being taken. Mom was told that two of my family would be transported by commercial airliner. Because my father hadn't flown since Vietnam and had sworn he'd never get on a plane again, my mother assumed my sister Jen would be at her side. My father had kept his promise by turning down vacations to

Hawaii, visiting us in the Middle East, and other opportunities to fly. But when he knew my life hung in the balance, there was nothing that could stop him from getting to me.

Family and friends took over all the details of getting my father an instant passport. They contacted the U.S. State Department for help and a passport was delivered to the house by 10:00 a.m. the next day. In addition, friends found my father a prescription for calming medications to help him with the flight.

By Friday morning, four days after the attack, my parents were escorted by Lufthansa personnel to the airplane.

Chris, David's good friend from seminary, was also at the airport to help with the press. Although he felt as emotional as anyone, he somehow flipped a switch and saved his grieving for later, becoming a strong support for my parents as they made preparations to leave.

At Landstuhl the first of many miracles happened in my recovery. A doctor who worked in Landstuhl had just returned from the Mosul CSH unit and would soon be leaving for Parkland Hospital in Dallas. He oversaw the big picture of my care. It was as if God had given me a head surgeon to work with doctors from Mosul to Landstuhl to the American trauma unit in Dallas.

After arriving in Germany, my parents turned right around and escorted me back to America on a Saturday. It had been five days since the attack, and when I was rushed to Parkland Hospital there was a full-scale trauma unit awaiting my arrival.

I was rushed into another surgery while my mother admitted me to the hospital. As she looked over the questions, she began sobbing when she got to the block that said, "Marital Status."

She was the first one to officially designate me as a widow. While I was in my coma, David had gone on to be with the Lord. I was a twenty-six-year-old widow and didn't even know it. The fear of my waking up to that news was overwhelming for my family. Would I continue to fight for my own life, knowing my best friend and husband wasn't there to share the future with me?

After the surgery, my mother was frantic I'd wake up before I'd had time to stabilize, and she would have to tell me about David. She couldn't bear to break my heart all over again. But my father stood by. He'd wanted to be the one to tell me the unbelievable and devastating news. It was why he went to Landstuhl in the first place, the one thing that got him over his fear of flying. He'd said, "If my baby wakes up, I'm going to be the one to explain what's happened. No one else."

The following Monday, a full week after the attack, nurses took the tube out that helped me breathe while I was unconscious, and I began waking up in waves, coming in and out of consciousness. I can't say I was ever truly awake during this time, but I received snippets of what was going on around me. I had little moments of awareness and understood I was back home in Dallas with my mama and daddy, a little girl safe in her parents' care. I wasn't cognizant enough, long enough, to ask for David, so for a while the news of his death wasn't an issue.

I stayed in the intensive care unit and the nurses began packing ice on me to wake me up. They began brushing my hair, which still contained dirt and shattered glass, and I felt my tender head being tugged and heard bits of glass hitting the floor. I smelled disinfectant but still was not completely aware. I had a vague sense of what was going on around me but wasn't participating. My mind wasn't capable of thinking about David or the attack as I was still finding my way to the surface.

I remember having weird dreams. I was aware of my mother's and father's presence, and I think I must have been hearing their conversation in the hospital room. They told me at one point that I'd asked for a cheeseburger, the food I missed most while in Iraq, but I remember little more than hearing their familiar voices around me.

Once I woke up briefly and looked around for my family. I knew I was back in America somehow, but I panicked at being alone. *How could my family leave me here all alone?* I thought. Of course, they had probably stepped out for a mere second, but in my mind, I was alone and no one cared. I was so scared to be without help. *Help me,* I thought. *Help me!* Just as in the moments after the attack, I tried to make my voice loud enough to be heard but couldn't. Panic welled up in my throat until I was able to get the attention of a passing nurse. She soothed me and explained my nurse would be in shortly. I soon passed out again.

During one of my waking episodes, I called out to my sister Jen, who sat in the room. "Psst! Psst! Let's get out of here," I said, like a high school senior ready to cut class.

"I can't get you out of here; I'll get in trouble," Jen said back to me. I'm sure I freaked her out, but I have no recollection of this conversation.

"Come on, no one will know," I continued, still lying in my bed without the ability to move. At the time, I was hooked up to a chest tube, multiple IV hookups, a foot vice that felt like torture, casts on both arms and my left leg, a vacuum machine on my leg to suck the wound outward, and I was still head-to-toe in bandages. It wasn't like I could actually get up and make a break for it even if Jen had been willing. Luckily, I went back to sleep before any damage was done.

The next time I woke up, I again tried to cry out for help but again could not make my voice do its job. Memories of the attack, being trapped in the truck, and my helplessness flooded in. For the first time, I started to relive the horrific events of March 15, 2004. There was a call button, but with both my arms immobilized in huge casts I couldn't reach for the button. My voice had no volume. I was like a mummy with no way to call out, and I panicked, fearful the bullets would start again.

I started hyperventilating and felt unable to breathe except in frantic, gasping breaths. I saw a nurse in the hallway. "Where am I?" I cried out as loud as I could.

The nurse came in and explained everything to me, that I was in Dallas and that my nurse would be there shortly. Just knowing I had a nurse allowed me to calm down and my pulse to drop back to "normal."

I was wrapped tightly and constrained in every way possible. I remember having the distinct feeling at this point that I was propped up somehow, like I was standing, and my body was tense like it had been that way for some time. I wanted to lie down and free myself. The leg machine was pumping—it felt excruciating and annoying.

"Nurse!" I called out to this woman in the hallway. "Can I lie down, please?" My tone was southern sweet, but my urgency came across.

She came in and laid a hand on me. "You are lying down, sweetie." As soon as she said it, I felt that it was true, but my mind was still playing tricks. I didn't know the difference between fact and fantasy in this eerie, strange place I found myself.

As the ice started taking effect and the breathing tube had been removed for a time, I started to gain alertness. I knew I was married but that my husband David wasn't at my side. I'd ask my Mother, "Where's David, Mama? Tell David to come in."

She would change the subject, and I would eventually fall back to sleep, unable to pursue the questioning any farther. My mom still cries just thinking about those times. It was so painful for her because she knew she had to battle for my life and my future, and that news of

David's death would have an excruciatingly stressful impact on me. More than once she had wanted to tell me about David, so I wouldn't think I'd been abandoned by him. But she wanted to make sure I was fully awake when I received the news. She didn't want me to drift to sleep only to wake up and relive the same horrifying conversation again. I must have somehow known enough not to press the issue too far, because I never pursued the conversation very adamantly.

When I'd wake up, David would be my first thought. "Now Mama, David's going to be awful shy about staying with you and Daddy; make sure you make him feel at home." I was really worried about him. If there was any situation that could reduce my boisterous husband to shyness, it was being one-on-one with my father.

Then, David's absence started to feel more real and strange, and I would cry out, "Mama, where's David? Is he mad at me? Why isn't he here?" I would sob, thinking about what I could have done to make him so mad at me.

My mom had to leave the room at this point; she couldn't keep denying me the truth, but I had one more surgery left and it was that morning. She didn't want me going under anesthesia under such stress, so she just kept putting off the inevitable conversation until I was done with all of the operations. *It will be soon*, she told herself.

I couldn't let the thought pass through my head that David might have died. I just couldn't go there, couldn't ask if he'd died. So while I think I had questions about David, they weren't as urgent as you might expect because I couldn't bear a negative answer. I hadn't survived all this to be without David, my best friend.

When I woke up after my final life-saving surgery (six of them, all told), the first thing I saw was a Texas A&M Aggie ring on the hand of the woman leaning over the metal railing. I leaned up and tried to take her hand to offer the traditional Aggie greeting: "Howdy, class of '99."

The nurse started to laugh and said, "Well, aren't you a maroon-blooded Aggie?"

"Look Mom, she's an Aggie," I said groggily. "And she has a *diamond* in her ring," I noted, a sign of an advanced degree. I then went back to sleep, but that was the first real conversation I remember well—that, and the dentist checking my teeth. After my surgery I remember wondering why they would have a dentist checking me. I remembered that I'd been hurt in the mouth, but I thought, "Surely, I have bigger issues than having a dental check-up here!" I didn't know of the possible dental problems that could have been a very real threat.

Eventually, I came out of the stupor for good, and they wheeled me from my last surgery recovery into ICU where my sister Jennifer was waiting. My sister and I are very close, and I knew I really needed the truth, so I said to her, "Jenna, Mama and Daddy are not telling me. Where is David?" I was steady enough now that I was annoyed that I didn't know where my husband was or why he wasn't in the room with me.

Jenna said, "Hold on, I'll go get Mom and Dad." She left the room and came back with my parents, and all three of them surrounded my bed and found a place they could lay a hand on me. Their concerned faces over me didn't tell me anything; I just thought news of David was forthcoming, and I was anxious.

My hands were both wrapped, so I couldn't hold their hands, but Daddy looked me in the eye and said, "David didn't make it, baby."

The room just spun. I tried to digest the news but it was so far out of my realm of comprehension. I cried out, "I've lost my best friend. I've lost my best friend! My baby!"

My family had all placed their hands on me, but I was completely wrapped like a mummy. When I most needed to, I couldn't hug them or even receive a hug for fear some tube or wire would get pulled loose. They were all right next to my bed, yet I felt so completely alone.

I had every expectation David would be there when I woke up. *They gave me every hope!* I didn't know if the doctors had lied, or if they really hadn't known he was that badly hurt. Truthfully, I really think no one knew how deep his wounds were.

When I finally caught my breath from sobbing, I asked, "How?"

"In the helicopter on the way to Baghdad," my mom answered. "They were transporting him from Mosul." As a surgical nurse, she knew they wouldn't have transferred him unless he'd been stable. David's death had to have shocked even the surgeons.

"Was the helicopter shot down?" I just couldn't grasp that David had died from his wounds in the attack. *I'd heard him talking! He was fine.*

"No, honey. David just arrested in the helicopter on the way to the hospital in Baghdad."

I just lay there and took it all in. I cried and cried over the loss, and I finally fell back to sleep, unable to believe that my best friend wasn't coming to my side in the hospital. *I was alone.* When I woke up, it took a while for it to sink in. I had a very real sense that he would just walk through the door.

With everything I had to do, I think my real grieving probably started later. But I would catch myself talking like he was still alive. (Sometimes I still do that, but it's getting better.) It really took me a couple of days to process that he hadn't made it. I just couldn't imagine it. David had not only survived, but actually thrived, in so many adverse situations; it was natural for me to expect this time to be no different.

As my mind continued to clear, I realized how long I'd been unconscious, and how long ago the attack had happened. Even now those days are still fuzzy, but it was over a week after the attack that I learned of David's passing.

"Where is David now?" I finally asked.

On the day that I woke up and found out about his death, David's family was having his funeral in Colorado—a memorial for someone I loved more than life, and I couldn't be there. I didn't get to plan his funeral or work through his death by thinking about what songs he'd want sung, what scripture he'd want read. I remember feeling so left out, that my husband was being buried without me there, and I sobbed some more. I cried to think that people were talking about his memory and I wasn't able to go and listen. This was the man who fought until the bitter end to save my life and I didn't get to thank him publicly for his life, his love, and our partnership.

Before the attack, David had been reading a book on being a proper husband and learning how to sacrifice for his wife. I can honestly say I wish he hadn't learned the lesson so well.

In tears, I asked my mother about the funeral, "Couldn't they wait, so I can be there?"

I was in the hospital for a month, and it was several months before I was able to travel. Of course they couldn't wait. But when I thought about his body in a grave in Colorado, thirteen hours away, I ached; my heart just ached. But David was pure Colorado and I was pure Texas. We'd lived in a foreign country to solve that dilemma, but deep down I knew David belonged in Colorado. It's what he would have wanted. He loved the mountains and the hiking and everything about the Colorado wilderness. He loved his parents and had so much in common with his dad in his love for the outdoors. That, and the Arab world, were his passions. *David would want that*, I thought, but it did little to help my broken heart. His grave is near the camp where he volunteered in high school and where all his best outdoor memories lived. I know he'd say that was, "Dadgum *kwayis.*" Darned good.

I wouldn't be an "everyday widow" and see the cemetery everyday, but I do wish I could be at his gravesite more often without the travel. I know David couldn't care less now, but the more selfish part of me missed an easy place to go and sit with my memory of him.

David's mother had struggled with what to do about the funeral and his burial place. She worried I would wake up and feel upset by her decisions. She was faced with such hard decisions regarding the funeral. Her son had died in Iraq; her daughter-in-law was fighting for her life in Texas. No one could have guaranteed that I was going to live. What other option did she have except to do the best she could? My mother-in-law made the right choices in a terrible situation. I just wished I could have been there. I wished I could have rejoiced in David's life and heard his friends tell their hilarious stories about the love of my life. He was the life of the party, a real-life Indiana Jones, and I wanted to hear everything and laugh at his memory and rejoice in a life so well-lived. I wanted to be there to do those things with the rest of the people who loved him. David and I had both been so moved by Genessa's funeral, especially the tributes given by her friends. I wanted to be there to hear others pay tribute to David's friendship and love of the Lord.

As it worked out, my sister was able to go to the memorial with her fiancé. She asked me before she left if I wanted to write something to be read at the service. Of course, I did, and I was so glad to be able to send something along with Jen. But imagine learning of your husband's death and being asked immediately to summarize your thoughts about his life! In my state of mental fuzziness, I was at a loss as to how to express my devotion to this man who literally laid down his life for my safety. I just opened my heart and let my thoughts flow and tried to think of scriptures that described David and that were special to him.

At the memorial service Jen began by saying, "These thoughts are based on Carrie's memories and reflections yesterday afternoon in her hospital room in Dallas. They include four passages of scripture that have been significant in their lives individually, and together, before the Lord."

I dictated to her what I wanted remembered about David: "David was a beautiful writer. He wrote wonderful e-mails. He kept journals. He wrote to me from the Sudan. We weren't allowed to date as Journeymen, but began an 'e-mail courtship.'" I had fallen in love with David's words. To this day, the comfort of his handwriting provides me with beautiful memories of how gifted he'd been with words.

I explained our courtship in Jen's memorial reading and gave the special scriptures that I felt brought us together. There were so many friends who barely knew of our courtship. We had been secretive for so long living in the Muslim world that it came as a shock to many that we were engaged and going to be married. Only those who knew us intimately expected it. I loved that I could finally share the story of our love.

Jennifer revealed how David was so unusually nervous at my parents' home for the Thanksgiving celebration. It took me a long time to figure out where the day was headed: roses, a cookie cake with "I love you" written in Arabic, and these passages from Ecclesiastes that culminated in a holiday marriage proposal:

> It's better to have a partner than go it alone.
> Share the work, share the wealth.
> And if one falls down, the other helps,

But if there's no one to help, tough!
Two in a bed warm each other.
Alone, you shiver all night.
By yourself you're unprotected.
With a friend you can face the worst.
Can you round up a third?
A three-stranded rope isn't easily snapped.

(ECCLESIASTES 4:9–12, MSG)

These were our wedding verses and a life verse on oneness. We had hoped to add our own third strand about God's presence in our marriage, but God obviously had a different plan.

My sister gave my final words for David at the graveside ceremony: "Iraq was a surprise to both of us. We went to Iraq in obedience to God. We were both expecting to go the Sudan. He was a good man, and you could tell by just knowing him.

"If I could just be as patient as David was with me . . . . What a mercy, there. He loved me. He just loved! He loved me spiritually. He wanted to be a godly leader in our home. He would ask, 'How do I lead?' So he went and got a book on it."

I chose this last passage from Revelation, not thinking about our life together, two precious years as partners in God's kingdom, but remembering where David is and what he is doing now.

I looked again. I saw a huge crowd, too huge to count. Everyone was there—all nations and tribes, all races and languages. And they were standing, dressed in white robes and waving palm branches, standing before the Throne and the Lamb and heartily singing:

Salvation to our God
on his throne!
Salvation to the Lamb!

(REVELATION 7:9–10, MSG)

My sister also read the following for me. "At the end of his earthly life, David's thoughts and actions were focused on me: getting help to remove me from the shattered vehicle, getting medical attention for me, denying his own wounds as he sought to take care of me. I thought, *how beautiful that David wanted to learn how to lead and bought a book on the subject.* God had given him the gift all along.

"We have lost a jewel—someone who is so precious to me, and we all knew it when we met him. Now that jewel and his flaming passion for Jesus, now that life is incense that burns before the altar of God."

David's memorial and the thought of him were always with me, but I had to put my grieving on the shelf to focus on getting better myself. I had a long way to go before I would be healthy enough to resume living—and remembering David. I still didn't have any information about why David died on the helicopter. I knew I would get it in due time, so I chose to let it go for the moment.

As my memory began to return and I realized what I'd been through in Mosul, I told my mom there were two people I needed to talk to. I needed to talk to a counselor who had cross-cultural missions experience—ideally, someone who had been to the Middle East. It would take that kind of person to help me process what I'd experienced.

I couldn't dump what I was feeling and thinking on my parents. I couldn't ask them to sit and listen to me debrief, and I knew they wouldn't understand a lot of what I would say or have answers to my questions related to the missionary experience. They were strug-gling just to help me get better. My mother lived at the hospital with me. She slept on a lumpy cushion no better than a camp cot. Besides the discomfort factor, nurses were in and out all hours of the night making necessary noise and keeping mom from a sound sleep. I couldn't put her through any more than she'd already endured. I just needed someone who understood the mission field. I needed to get everything off my chest.

Obviously, I was an emotional wreck, and I was beginning to have visions that scared me. I needed someone who understood the Bible well, to interpret what was happening inside me. When I'd close my eyes, I'd see movies so real I couldn't shut them off. They weren't dreams (because I wasn't asleep), but visions, rolling like a reel before my eyes. That's when I asked her to call the second person.

"And I need to talk to Beth, Mom."

I'd met Beth Moore in Israel when she'd come to videotape a Bible study series. I knew she was a diligent student of Scripture, and I thought she could shed some light on the visions and pictures I was seeing in my mind. I'd grown attached to her in the two short weeks we'd toured Israel together and was blessed enough to worship and fellowship with her. During our time together in Israel, I observed how much Beth genuinely cares for people. So I never doubted she would make herself available to me in my time of need. Beth came to my mind and I asked for her, because I intuitively knew she would *want* to try to help me understand the visions.

In the Middle East, anything you do to call attention to yourself as a Christian is frowned upon. It's almost like we live as secret agents, afraid to reveal our real identity. Beth's group allowed me to identify myself as a Christian away from the day-to-day drudgery of scrubbing bathrooms and floors. I will always be grateful for that time and her friendship for that reason. I just knew she was the one to help me understand the visions. If I could understand them, I thought I could be free of them. And I needed to be able to close my eyes and sleep without being kept awake by the movies playing on the inside of my eyelids.

My mom assured me she'd get in touch with both people, the counselor and Beth, and I started to relax. A security detail had been blocking the elevators in the hospital to keep reporters from getting to my room. Though the authorities hadn't released details about where I was, they'd posted policemen to ensure that no journalists were allowed to sneak into my room.

I couldn't believe that we'd been on the news. "David and me?" I asked, astonished.

"Over and over again," came the reply.

Thinking about lying in a hospital room with policemen to protect me did nothing to settle my mind. I wasn't in a place where I felt safe yet, and I still hadn't come to grips with the fact that my beloved wouldn't be coming back, or the horrifying details of what we shared. I was still reliving the terror, still feeling death surround me.

Journalists had descended upon the town like a plague. They were calling our house and were camped out front with their news trucks. They were desperately trying to find out what hospital I was in so they could be the first to get the interview.

David's best friend, Chris McKinney, came to our rescue from seminary where he'd attended with David. Chris is built like a good-sized linebacker with a commanding presence and Southern charm. Because my parents still needed to receive important phone calls from the mission board and hospitals overseas, they had no choice but to answer the phones. Chris stepped in and became the liaison for the news media. He answered the barrage of phone calls and filled my parent's doorway with his barrel chest when necessary. Chris would go out and plant himself on the lawn and ask the media to be respectful, and for the most part they were. But they still had a job to do and they weren't going to quit trying.

During my stay in the hospital I talked with Larry and Jean Elliott's children at length. I was able to tell them that their parents had not suffered for long, and how much I came to love them after only knowing them a short time. I felt an immediate bond with all three of their adult children. I felt they understood my loss because they were experiencing a tremendous loss as well. They were glad to know their parents went together and quickly. The Elliotts had always said they'd hoped life would end that way for them—together, just as their ministry had been. It did my heart good to talk with other people who felt the loss so intently and to hear that the Elliotts, too, had heeded God's call with no regrets or fears about where it might lead.

I had to rely on God's sovereignty in the deaths of so many committed missionaries. I truly believed that David, the Elliotts, and Karen Watson had been called home after their time on earth was done. I didn't feel for a minute that their lives were randomly taken any more than I believed I had survived by chance. I knew David would never have been happy being a seminary student or being a pastor in a place that didn't involve Arab Muslims and adventure or even in a place where there were many other missionaries readily available and willing to go. He wanted to be in a place without many believers, where he could shine a light into the darkness. When 9/11 happened, he felt the Arab Muslims needed him more than ever, and he was anxious to get to work. Living out his passions was more important to him than his life, and that made me proud.

The Elliotts were a powerful witness to that passion. They could have retired stateside, thrown in the towel on their life's work.

Heaven knows they deserved it, but they listened and went to Iraq. Before they left the States, they visited their longtime home church, Baptist Temple Church in Reidsville, North Carolina. Of course, people had questions, and if you haven't been called it's impossible to understand why people like the Elliotts would go. George Fox, the pastor of their home church, quoted the Elliotts: "You could die in traffic in Raleigh. It's safer to be in the center of God's will."

The Elliott's sent an e-mail to family and friends shortly after they arrived in Iraq. "We are happy to be here and our call has been confirmed," they said. "We love you all." In my heart, even as I tried to deal with the pain of the loss, I knew David and my friends were standing at the foot of the throne, hearing from their Father, "Well done, good and faithful servants."

CHAPTER EIGHTEEN

The Road to Recovery

As I became more aware of my surroundings, I apparently developed a compulsive need to talk. If you were in my hospital room you would hear what was on my mind at that moment. Perhaps it was avoiding the daily reality of being a widow, but talking became my saving grace.

Paranoia became an issue. I had a strong sense that someone was out to get me, and being so completely immobile in my hospital bed there was nothing I could do to escape. I felt the same way I'd felt in the truck. I had no ability to defend myself, no way out. My heart would race at the ding of the elevator bell, and I'd wake in a sweat sometimes.

Part of the problem was knowing that the news media were looking for me; knowing there were policemen at the elevators made me imagine there were people on the other side of the elevator doors who wanted to hurt me. That all seems so irrational now, but at the time it was real. I began to wonder if I'd ever forget everything I'd seen. I was so glad I'd closed my eyes during most of the attack, yet I knew I had been permanently imprinted with many of the images that day and would have to deal with them for the rest of my life.

My visions were becoming more frequent and I hoped that I'd hear from Beth Moore soon. In addition to the visions, one night as I lay in bed I began hearing the sound of men's voices singing—like an old-time gospel choir. I thought at first it must be coming from an adjoining hospital room. They sang beautifully—the sound of their voices relaxed me and the conviction with which they sang encouraged me. My mother was already asleep on her cot and I knew she was tired—but I so wanted her to hear this beautiful music. I thought she might go to the room next door and ask them to come to my room, or at least tell them how much I was enjoying listening to them.

I called to my mother and asked her if she could hear the singing.

"No, baby," she said.

I listened more closely to the words: "Lord, we thank You for the cross, we thank You for our lives . . . Lord, we praise You with our hearts."

I thought, *Wow, this is a group that can sing!* "I want them in my room, Mama," I said. "Mama, can you hear it?"

"No, I don't hear it," Mom said.

"Are you sure? I *know* I am not crazy! I'm not!" I then told her the words of the song and where it was coming from. My mom got up and put her head against the wall.

"No, I don't hear it, baby. I'm sorry."

"Well, me too," I told her. "You're missing out."

"Well, enjoy it, baby." She climbed back onto her bed, and said, "Maybe it's the Lord allowing this to be sung over you. Relax and enjoy it."

The music sounded like it came from the room behind my bed. I heard it so regularly that I learned the words and would sing along with it. I heard it for the rest of my stay in the hospital—but I was the only one; no one else ever heard it. I believe it was one of God's sweet mercies to His suffering child. Zephaniah 3:17 (NIV) says, "The Lord your God is with you, he is mighty to save. He will take great delight in you, he will quiet you with his love, he will rejoice over you with singing."

Our Lord gave His wounded child a new song. In the quietness of my room, I would tap my right foot (the one that was free from bandages and braces) with the music as if I had been listening to a tape player or a live choir. I find it interesting that the first line in the song was, "Lord, I thank You for the cross." How fitting that God wanted me to rejoice in my salvation, in the cross, where our victory was won.

To me, it became a victory song—not just in my life, but for all of us. By His cross we can be thankful; by His cross we can praise Him. It also takes me back and reminds me of our Father's loving kindness. In a truly dark, sad, and scary time, He opened my ears to hear a new song.

Because no one else could hear what I was hearing, I asked my friend, Amy Nobles, to come to the hospital and set the words to music for me. I wanted everyone to hear the beautiful song God was causing to be sung over me.

My physical therapy had started, but I still couldn't lift my arms more than two or three inches off the bed. One night, I dreamed I was hearing the song "Worship the King," the chorus of which says, "With my hands lifted high, I will worship and sing. With my hands lifted high, I come before You rejoicing. With my hands lifted high to the sky, when the world wonders why I'll just tell them I'm loving my King"—and I began lifting my arms in praise to the Lord! Somehow, as I dreamed, my arms overcame their physical weakness, and I could raise them all the way off the bed. Then, at my next physical therapy session, they felt like they were glued to the mattress.

My mother just laughed, saying, "All right, baby, if you want to do your physical therapy with God in your sleep, that's fine with me."

After talking to the counselor I began to feel the weight lift a little at a time. The right people finally got in touch with Beth Moore and she came to see me. It was less than a week since I'd asked to see her, but with the visions going on incessantly it felt like an eternity. Beth had heard about me on television, but they were using my married name so she never connected that I was the one involved in the attack.

The day she was to come, my sister Jen helped me prepare. She bought me a set of new clothes and helped me get dressed. I wasn't about to wear a hospital gown when Beth came to see me. We had given Beth the alias name she had to ask for in order to get past the guards in the hospital, and when she finally got there and entered the room I was overjoyed to see her. I couldn't believe that she was there—the last time I had seen her was a few years before and thousands of miles away in Israel.

So much had happened since I had last been with her. It was a blessing to be able to tell her about the man I met and married. To share a bit of David with her allowed me to unburden myself in a different way than I had with those who joined me in grieving for him. Beth gave me words of encouragement to help me deal with my grief.

I explained the visions I was having to Beth. In one, I saw people running around chaotically without direction or purpose, not knowing where they were going. In another I saw people running purposefully in one direction, without any fear. And in yet another I saw people walking tiredly toward a man whom I knew was Jesus. As they approached Him, some would walk around Him and keep on walking, while others would stop and allow Jesus to embrace them. He would release them after an embrace and turn them around, setting them on a new path; they would walk away from Him with renewed strength and purpose, confident of where they were headed.

Beth thought my visions meant that God has a purpose for us. He wants us to know and walk in His purpose, but the only way to do that is to embrace Jesus and allow Him to set us on the path He chooses for us. She said that the visions confirm that some will choose Jesus and run hard with a purpose, while others will go on without him, running in chaos, doing whatever they feel is right. Hearing Beth's words about the visions reminded me that God has a purpose for my life. God was not surprised by the terrorist attack in Mosul, Iraq. He is not a God of chaos but a God of purpose—*regardless of how things may sometimes appear.* I needed to continue to run hard on the path where Jesus had placed me, just as my beloved David finished his life running hard on the path Jesus had chosen for him.

As I began to focus on my injuries and getting over them, I was shocked to learn I'd been hit at least twenty-two times by bullets and shrapnel. The shrapnel actually does more harm than the bullets, due to its tunneling and tearing effect. It burns tissue from its hot, molten state. As much as my body hurt, I wouldn't take the morphine the nurses offered. I hated the way it made me feel and I hated not being in control of my mind. It was the one thing I had that I could control, so after days of my not punching the button to release the drug, my nurse finally dismantled the IV and gave in to my stubbornness.

My left leg had been shot from the left side, just below my knee. The bullet shattered the tibia, the larger lower leg bone, and took everything with it—the skin, the nerves, and the bone itself—leaving a gaping hole as it exited. My left leg was hooked up to a suction machine constantly and I felt the weight of its damage daily. In the Iraq unit, they'd attached an external stabilizing device, which looked like Tinkertoy® components, and made me feel like a living Erector

Set®. At first it was difficult for me to view. In order to help me cope with looking at the metal attached to my leg, I found humor in the fact that it looked like a Tinkertoy®, so I came to call my leg "Tink."

Another bullet went through my upper left leg above the knee. Fortunately, although that bullet caused significant muscle damage, it just missed my femoral artery.

Another bullet on my right leg just scraped the lower part of my thigh, not causing any interior damage. I had a cat-scratch type scar from that one.

On my left hand, I lost all the fingers except my middle finger and my thumb. Jen and I jokingly call it, "Flick." But I have to admit—the damage to my hands upset me more than any of my other injuries. I'd always been a little prideful about my small, dainty hands, and now they bore the most obvious of my scars. Add to that a shattered bone in my right arm and a bullet to the joint in my left elbow, and I was left with two useless arms during recovery. Fortunately, the bullet in my left arm stopped at the joint, or I would have lost the arm completely.

The doctors inserted a plate that runs the length of my forearm before closing the wound in my right arm. I have a long, red caterpillar-like scar on my arm. I understand that vanity is useless at this point (or anytime) but I am very self-conscious. Once, after recovering, I was sitting in an airport thinking about how many people have scars internally from conflicts in life. I wished that my scars weren't on the outside because they provoke so many questions. And the questions make me relive my worst nightmare over and over again. The questions are understandable, and I can't expect they'll ever stop. But I want to be free of the pain involved in recounting what happened. I believe I'll reach that goal in God's time.

In addition to my limbs, my right ear was pelted by pieces of shrapnel, along with a bullet. Two more bullets, and more shrapnel, hit my face. One went through my cheek and was probably the bullet I spit out in the truck. Miraculously, it did little damage to my gums or teeth. The second bullet entered my cheek near my smile line and broke the septum in my nose where it connects to the lip, which is why I couldn't breathe after the attack. This bullet fractured my mandible and was the reason for countless CT scans. The doctors simply couldn't believe that there was no brain damage.

Doctors later said the slight damage to my face was miraculous. I have just a small scar above my smile line and one at my cheek, giving me a new dimple. To look at me now, one would never know what my face had been through. I owe it to God's grace working through talented surgeons.

Besides all of the obvious limb damage, one bullet got me in the right chest. It skidded across my ribs, breaking them as it went, but missed all major organs, and exited beneath my left breast. Doctors couldn't believe that bullet hadn't reached the organs, and in the sixty-seventh CSH unit in Iraq they took several x-rays, because there was a shadow that showed a mass in my chest. Doctors, believing that the chest bullet had punctured the sac around my heart, pried open my sternum to get a closer look at the mass, leaving a huge open-heart scar down the middle of my chest. Completely unrelated to my gunshot wounds, the mass on the x-rays turned out to be a large tumor growing off my bronchial tree. While doctors drained the tumor at Landstuhl and took a biopsy (from which we hadn't yet received the results), my mother decided she couldn't worry about a tumor in the midst of all my other medical problems. She handed that one over to God and left it in His hands.

When they pulled my chest tube at Parkland Hospital in Texas, a doctor came in to speak to my mother while they were doing another

MRI. He wore a camouflage surgical cap, a remnant from his days in the field, and said to my mother, "Good news, the tumor is benign."

So while my prognosis was improving every day, we were still awaiting David's autopsy report. He'd died the day after the attack at 3:00 a.m. American time. He was being moved by helicopter from Mosul's U.S. Army hospital unit to another army hospital in Baghdad.

All of the surgeons, men who saw the worst wounds possible, believed that David would live. Surgeons who care for soldiers' combat injuries are the best in the business. They know what they're doing. When we received assurance that David would survive his injuries, I know they thought it to be true. God definitely said, "I'm taking him." It was David's time.

My scars on the outside are nothing compared to the bullet and shrapnel tunnels that still exist in my system. When I go through an airport security system it lights up like a Christmas tree because there is so much metal still in my body. For weeks in the hospital, my body literally shed metal shavings as my system worked them out. My body was covered with black scabs from the shrapnel, as if you'd thrown water in a hot pan of oil and it had exploded all over me. Slowly, my body has eliminated a great deal of the metal, but it will never be completely gone.

I will always have visual reminders, as well as the physical and mental scars, to remind me of my brush with death. Worst of all, I will live this life without David. For those of us left here to grieve, it will be a long road, filled with hard memories, yet graced with thanksgiving for the time we had with those now gone.

My immediate future holds several more operations including one on my right hand, where a piece of shrapnel is still lodged between my forefinger and my thumb. It's painful and so it will be removed. Additionally, I'll also have another operation to straighten my middle finger, the only finger besides my thumb I have on my left hand. It needs a bit more skin grafting to straighten it out, improve the movement, and make it look more natural. I'll have more surgery on my leg to improve mobility, as well. The end of my physical recovery is in sight—just a few more bends in the road to go around.

I hope to visit Israel again, to see the Arab family who adopted me while I was there. Will I ever go back to Iraq? Maybe—I can't say for certain. I do hope to conquer the fear that I live with when I hear a sharp sound or see something out of the ordinary. (I have hit the ground for cover when someone dropped something in the grocery store.)

My husband, David, lived his life like King David—with a whole heart for God, like Saint Paul on a constant missionary quest, and like Daniel, who feared nothing when in the lion's den. Like those saints of old, David followed God when the outcome wasn't certain. May we all strive to love others as David McDonnall did. I believe the world will be a better place if we do.

We shouldn't fear death in Christ. We have nothing to be afraid of when we serve a sovereign God who is very much in control of this world. It's time His children start living like they believe it. To all who suffer for Him, it is a gift to know the fellowship of His sufferings.

I live my life without David, but am grateful for the time I had with him. The world is not our place of rest; it is a time to work and follow hard after Jesus. When we get home, we can rest. But for now, God is calling His children to share the gospel of the cross, the power of our Holy Father; it's time we obediently follow Him. May we all live our lives in a manner worthy of the calling we have received in Christ Jesus. May we live lives we will never regret.

AFTERWORD

It's been a year without David. I've made it through the anniversaries, holidays, and the birthdays. All of these moments I planned to have David by my side, and yet I've watched them slip by much differently than I had imagined. I won't sugarcoat the fact that it's been excruciating, and I'm constantly aware of his absence. I miss our life together. I miss the possibilities of what I thought our future together might hold. I'll mourn for the rest of my life, but I am thankful for the time I spent as David McDonnall's best friend and wife.

We had a true love story that began the day we met. Some might call it fate; others said we were made for each other. I desired to share our story, our romance, not so you might say, "Wow, what great people," but that you would stand with me in awe of the one true and living God whom we can call Father.

Yes, I miss my husband. And yes, I mourn the loss of three dear friends. But, I do not grieve as those without hope (1 Thessalonians 4:13), because my hope rests in Jesus. God has been very near, and in His presence I have found the strength to rejoice in His faithfulness.

I can't help but wonder if this is how men in chains found the strength to sing and what gave Paul the strength to get up and carry on after being stoned and left for dead.

I hope this story of two of His very ordinary children will cause you to take hold of Jesus and live this life hard in reckless abandonment to all He truly is.

—CARRIE MCDONNALL

Lord, I Praise You
Words and Music by
Amy Nobles and Carrie McDonnall

Lord, I thank You for the cross
Choir: Lord, I praise You
Lord, I thank You with my heart
Choir: Lord, I praise You
I thank You with my life
Choir: Lord, I praise You
I'll thank You with this song
Choir: Lord, I praise You

Unison Chorus—
Lord, I praise Your name
Give You thanks and
Lift up holy hands
Without shame
I will proclaim
Jesus' name
in all the earth

So I'll sing among the nations
Choir: Hallelujah!
For great is Your love
Choir: Glory! Glory!
It's higher than the heavens
Choir: Higher! Higher!
It reaches to the sky!
Choir: Lord, I praise You!

ACKNOWLEDGMENTS

To the people who helped make this book happen:

Integrity Publishers, thank you for being willing to hear this story and then desiring to see our Lord glorified in its telling. Thank you for your hard work.

Kristin, I am sure you raised an eyebrow when they approached you with this project! Thank you for not dismissing it and for following Christ's lead when everything else seemed to say differently. You are a gifted writer, and I am honored that you were willing to enter into this story and tell it from the inside looking out.

Jeana, what a godsend! Wow! You are my voice when I don't know what to do and my shield when I need one. Thank you for taking such good care of this project and watching over me. You have brought glory to our Father by diligently doing the work He has given you.

To the thousands of people who took time to send cards and letters of condolence and encouragement:

You didn't know me, and yet you acted. Thank you for your prayers for me and my family and for your faithfulness to pray.

To all the men and women who spent countless hours in surgery with my husband and me:

Thank you for your skill, your endurance, and for offering comfort. To the men and women who knelt at my husband's bedside in prayer and who held his hand when I couldn't, thank you for caring for him. To the nurses, doctors, and staff at Landstuhl Regional Medical Center in Germany, thank you for watching over me and taking care of my family. Thank you to the nurse who stayed after her shift to soak my right hand to rid it of the blood and debris under my nails. To the chaplain who cried with my family and offered support in a foreign land. To all who went above and beyond, knowing I may never know of it, thank you. Harriett and family, thank you for taking my family in as part of your own. It was good to hear that fellow Aggies were there to look after each other! Gig 'em! To my nurses, doctors, and the staff at Parkland Hospital in Dallas, thank you for not only caring for my health but for my family and being considerate of what we were going through. To the seventh floor nurses and staff, thank you, thank you, thank you. You not only did your job incredibly well, but you went above and beyond and became my friends. You brought laughter to my room, encouraged me in my healing, and understood and respected the grief I was suffering. At a time that could have been much more painful, you helped ease the pain both physically and emotionally. May the Lord return to you the blessing you have been to my family and me. To my torture-loving friends (also known as physical and occupational therapists), thank you for having mercy and yet pushing me when I needed to be pushed. I hope I never have to be in your hands again, but I know that because of those hands, I am able to move what was once immovable! I am incredibly thankful.

To my "angels" in desert camo:

Thank you for coming to our aid, for seeing our hurt and need, and making us feel safe. To those warriors who knelt before the throne of grace on our behalf, words can't express my gratitude. To my "focus man" Tim, I pray for you and your family. Thank you for your tenderness and comfort in the midst of my darkest hour. I will never forget you.

To the students and staff at Southwestern Theological Seminary:

Thank you for praying for me and my family, and for honoring David's memory. To Dr. and Mrs. Patterson, thank you for your support of my family, visiting us while I was in the hospital, and allowing me to hold a memorial service for David on campus. To Drs. Crutchley and Garrett, thank you for bringing encouraging words to my hospital bed, praying over me, and breaking open Scriptures to pour over a wounded heart. Thank you for your messages of mercy and grace.

To the fellowship of churches in my life:

Each of you is dear to my heart and has played a central role in my growth in the faith. Lake Highland, thank you for your prayers and support during the all-night prayer vigil following the attack, for supporting my family, and bringing comfort at my bedside. I will never forget the place where I was raised on the truth and love of Jesus. Central in College Station, Texas, thank you for your prayers and support and for my other education in college, lead by Brothers Chris and Kevin. Your teaching and leadership grounded me in my faith. Travis Avenue, thank you for your prayers and support; to Dr. and Mrs. Dean for encouraging me at my bedside and offering scripture to help heal my heart; to my Sunday School class for sending clothes and thinking of the small things. To my family at Lake Pointe Church, thank you for your prayers and silent support; to Pastor Steve and JR, your teaching of the truth has graced my life in a powerful way. The Lord has used it to help me heal. Merritt (a sister that tells it like is!) and my ABF, thank you for ministering to my mom in her darkest hour and for your prayers and encouragement each Sunday. You continue to lift me up and encourage me.

To my friends:

What an honor to thank my friends this way. I love each of you, and these words do not come close to touching the thankfulness I have for all of you.

"I thank my God in all my remembrance of you."

They say you find out who your real friends are during a crisis. My friends surrounded my family and me—offering help, laughter, and tears. I would like to thank Laurie, Erica, Jennifer, Jessica, and Bridget for relieving my family of night duty when I was in the hospital. Your willingness to help me get through those first hurdles was true friendship. Thank you for praying over me as I tried to drift off to sleep, for serving a hurt sister, and for continuing to be there for me. You have radiated the love of Jesus. To my friends who visited me, you brought laughter and Freebirds. Thank you to Ms. Libby for the laughter and joy your friendship adds to my life. Thanks for bringing me some Pat in the hospital and for lovin' *Songs About Texas* with me. To Holly (get off the porch!): who knew when we traipsed through Galilee we would be here together? Thank you for your laughter. To Susan and Jeremy, for extending the comfort the Lord has poured into each of your lives and for sharing with me what you have learned in your own healing process. Yes, Jeremy, I agree with your tears of joy, we serve a merciful and loving Father.

To Rebekah, for sitting at my bedside and putting chapstick on my blistered lips. Your thoughtfulness and comfort were like healing water upon my broken heart (Gig 'em!). To Amy for bringing your beautiful gift of music to my hospital room, for being willing to complete the song "Lord, I Praise You," and for taking a few road trips with me to share your love of Jesus (Gig 'em!). To Chris, for answering a call in the middle of the night to come to the aid of my family and for busing all the girls back and forth from the hospital. David counted you as a best friend—someone he could count on. I will never forget watching the antics of "Joe Fred and Billy Fred" or "Gretchen.") To Mr. B., it did my heart good to see one of my mentors and his wife visit with me and laugh at my mishaps in high school FFA! Thank you for your wisdom over the years, for putting up with me in high school, for encouraging me in college, and for your continued encouragement. You have influenced many lives with your knowledge of agriculture and desire to honor Jesus in your teaching; your quiet and stern faith has encouraged me in my faith despite surrounding influences. Thank you, Mr. Benson. Eddie and family—I'm struggling with where to start. Eddie, I hope you know how much you meant to David and how much he loved you. He explained to me once how much your relationship meant to him; you were second only to his Dad. He saw you as a friend and father figure. I am so thankful you were there for my family that fateful day. I know it wasn't easy, yet you stayed, prayed, and brought laughter and wisdom at times when both were hard to find. Thank you for sticking with me, even now. Myrla, thank you for helping with this project, offering wisdom, and letting me borrow from that knowledge. Thank you, Eddie and Myrla, for being my visionaries and motivators. Boys, thanks for letting me into your world, I pray you each would follow hard after Jesus, surpassing the faith and

obedience of your parents. I love you guys! Dr. Martin, thank you
for coming to my hospital room and helping me through the begin-
nings of the grieving process and emotional healing. Thank you for
letting me cry, offering wisdom and guidance through the
Scriptures, and feeling free to laugh at "the idiot in the truck." You
have been my Titus ("But God, who comforts the downcast,
comforted us by the coming of Titus" 2 Corinthians 7:6). Beth
Moore, I am thankful the Lord caused our paths to cross years
before this event. Thank you for your wisdom, guidance, and love
for our Father and His Word. Thank you for being "real" as you
share it with us, and for spurring us on to a deeper love for His
Word. Thank you for coming to my bedside in the hospital, to offer
encouragement and guidance. Thank you for continuing to be "in
my corner," offering advice on this road I am traveling. I am blessed
and honored.

To the family of Karen Watson:

Thank you for your cards and letters of support. Many people
have come to me with tears in their eyes and smiles on their faces
and said, "I knew Karen." That's all they need to say. I can hear the
pride in their voices and see the love they have for her. Their
response is a testimony to what a wonderful woman she was and
what an incredible life she lived. She was living out a faith that
impacted so many people, not because of her death but because of
her LIFE! Karen's life changed so many people long before the events
of March 15, 2004. I know she changed mine. She was so willing to
serve her Lord, even in the midst of uncertainties. How many times
in life do we have certainties? That's a lesson I learned from my
friend Karen. I am so sorry for your loss and pray that you would
continue to find comfort in our Lord.

To Karen's other family, Valley Baptist Church, thank you for your support, prayers, and love. You have taken me in as one of your own, and I am grateful.

To the families of Larry and Jean Elliott:

You have all surrounded me as if I was one of you. I feel as though I have gained a family. I am so sorry for your loss. Larry and Jean were beautiful people. Larry was hilarious with his boisterous laugh; your mom so soothing with her gracious spirit and sweet smile. Both held such a passion to serve our Lord. After meeting all of you, I see you are living out and passing on their legacy. During the time I knew Larry and Jean, I fell in love with them and was looking forward to getting to know them more. I am still looking forward to it.

To the Miller family:

I am proud of how we remain together, even after we have grown so much. Paw-Paw would be proud! Thank you for surrounding my parents, for praying for us, for helping out wherever they needed you. Aunt Jeannie, thank you for being such a support for Momma and for me. Thank you and Uncle Randy for being such a strong part of my spiritual growth. I bet you never realized that picking up a child on Wednesdays for church would have such an impact. Thank you.

To the McDonnall family:

Donna and Bruce, thank you for your continued support and help. I know it hasn't been easy. Thank you for being here for me, even through the pain of losing your son. Thank you for your prayers and your love. I love you.

To my family:

You are amazing! Granted, I'm biased and I've always felt this way about you. We're the type of family that circles the wagons when one of us needs a hand. So when I think of all you've done, it makes me thankful . . . incredibly so.

Jenna is not only my big sis but my hair stylist (Sister can do some good hair!), my massage therapist (always a lovely quality in a sister), and most importantly my friend. Thank you for loving David like a brother (y'all had too much fun ganging up on me!), for staying with me on those dark nights in the hospital (I didn't get you kicked out after all with my crazy schemes!), and for your encouragement as we grieve together.

Nick (my brother-in-law), welcome to the family! You have entered at your own risk! Thank you for your quiet support of my sister, the kids, and my parents. Your behind-the-scenes support has not gone unnoticed, and we couldn't have done as well without you.

Kaitlyn (my niece), my Possum! I love you, little girl! David loved you! I am so proud of who you are becoming. You have such a strong sense of doing the right thing and a great determination to see it done. I am thankful for your young faith in Jesus. Let no one deter you from following Him and what you know to be true. Keep striving after Him, for when you seek Him you will find Him. There is no other more satisfying. I pray you continue to grow up in Him and that you will live this life not settling for less than what Jesus desires for you.

Dayton, you're an awesome nephew! I love you so much! You know David loved you too. I hope one day you will know what an honorable man he was and let his memory serve as an example for your faith and how you will choose to live. I pray you, too, will live this life hard, not settling for anything less than what Jesus desires for your life. Run hard after Him, Bubba, for when you seek Him, you will find Him.

Momma and Pop, you have always supported my desire to live among the nations and never questioned my sanity or my calling. I know it wasn't easy, but you remained encouragers to both David and me. The words "Thank You" seem weak in comparison to all your support. Even when your hearts were broken, you stood strong for your daughter—to help her heal, grieve, and turn to Jesus for strength. Many people have wondered how I came by my strength. It comes first from above and secondly because that kind of strength was lived out as an example before me. Thank you for raising your girls to have a little steel in them and for your examples of faith as followers of Jesus Christ. I love you, and as always, I'll carry on . . . .

CARRY ON MINISTRIES

Out of the tragedy that occurred on March 15, 2004, the Lord has awakened many people to His desire to make Himself known among the nations.

Carry On Ministries seeks to continue in that task—to help awaken the church to God's global purpose, to help ease the burdens of those who are already serving among the nations, and to mobilize God's people to unity so we might "stand firm in one spirit and one mind striving together for the faith of the Gospel."

If you would like more information on how to invite Carrie McDonnall to share at your event or more information about Carry On Ministries, please visit Carrie at
www.carryonministries.org